InstaKnits
for Baby

Melissa Leapman

Stackpole Books
Essex, Connecticut
Blue Ridge Summit, Pennsylvania

STACKPOLE BOOKS

An imprint of Globe Pequot, the trade division of The Rowman & Littlefield Publishing Group, Inc.
4501 Forbes Blvd., Ste. 200
Lanham, MD 20706
www.rowman.com

Distributed by NATIONAL BOOK NETWORK
800-462-6420

Copyright © 2023 Melissa Leapman
Photography © 2023 Gale Zucker

British Library Cataloguing in Publication Information available

Library of Congress Cataloging-in-Publication Data available

ISBN 978-0-8117-7174-0 (paper : alk. paper)
ISBN 978-0-8117-7175-7 (electronic)

∞™ The paper used in this publication meets the minimum requirements of American National Standard for Information Sciences—Permanence of Paper for Printed Library Materials, ANSI/NISO Z39.48-1992.

First Edition

To Abigail and Charlie,

the greatest grandnieces ever!

CONTENTS

PROJECTS

Less Than Five Hours   3

Five to Ten Hours 53

Ten to Twenty Hours 77

More Than Twenty Hours 107

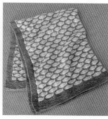

RESOURCES

INTRODUCTION

If you're like me, your life is overloaded with work, family, and social obligations, without enough hours in the day to fit everything in. (No wonder I never seem to make it to the gym!) When I do find a way to squeeze in a few precious hours of knitting, another baby shower or birthday party invite arrives. (Goodbye, personal knitting!)

Here's the book we all need: a collection of 30 fresh, easy-to-knit, and social media-worthy projects for the adorable littles in our lives, from newborns to 24 months of age. Even more exciting, nearly half of them take less than five hours to stitch. (Talk about Insta-knitting!)

To make the book easy to use, the projects are arranged in chapters based on the time commitment needed to finish them.

> Do you carpool to swim meets or soccer practice? Good! You can make use of that waiting time and knit the plush beach ball on page 26 in just one sitting.

> Have you promised yourself one afternoon every weekend to spend on your craft? You can whip out the sweet, stuffed bunny on page 67 before dinner!

> Does your family binge-watch Netflix on long holiday weekends? Turn them into your personal stitching time! You can crank out the toasty All Heart Blanket on page 112 by the opener of Season 3.

You can tackle most of these designs using only basic knitting skills, but if something looks unfamiliar, refer to the handy Resources section in the back of the book. Photos demonstrate nearly every technique from the cast-on to the bind-off and all the fun stuff in between.

Once you have finished a project, I'd love to see it! Please use #InstaKnitsForBaby and the individual hashtag shown on the project page on your social media and tag me. I'll gladly share it. Who knows, maybe your post (with your beautiful Little One modeling, of course) will go viral! (Hello, Hollywood scouts!)

#InstaKnitsForBaby #InstaKnits
#MakersGonnaMake #KnittingforBaby
#BabyKnits @Melissa.Leapman

LESS THAN FIVE HOURS

Do you want (or need) to crank out a last-minute baby gift? Choose a project from this chapter of the book. Each design can be completed while you're tied to the house during the cable-guy installation window.

#QuickKnits
#SqueezingInYourMeTime

Cute Caterpillar

#InstaKnitsForBaby_CuteCaterpillar

TIME TO KNIT 3 hours

FINISHED MEASUREMENTS

Length: 9½ in/24 cm
Width: 1½ in/4 cm

MATERIALS

- Berroco *Comfort Worsted* (#3 medium weight; 50% nylon/ 50% acrylic; each approximately 3½ oz/100 g and 210 yd/193 m), 1 ball each of Pearl #9702 (A), Robin's Egg #9714 (B), Peach #9704 (C), Raspberry Sorbet #9728 (D), and Buttercup #9712 (E)
- Knitting needles, US size 7 (4.5 mm) or size needed to obtain gauge
- Double-pointed knitting needles, US size 7 (4.5 mm)
- 1 yd/1 m of black yarn or embroidery floss
- Fiberfill stuffing

GAUGE

In Stockinette Stitch, 20 stitches and 28 rounds = 4 in/10 cm, blocked.

To save time, take time to check gauge.

I-Cord (Over 3 Stitches)

Pattern Row (RS): Using 2 double-pointed knitting needles, knit across. *Do not turn. Slide to the beginning of the row.*

Repeat the Pattern Row.

> **NOTE:** *This design is worked flat and seamed.*

CATERPILLAR

HEAD

With A, cast on 9 stitches.

Row 1 (WS): Purl across.

Row 2: *K1, M1 (page 144); repeat from the * across, ending with k1—17 stitches.

Row 3: Purl across.

Row 4: *K2, M1; repeat from the * across, ending with k1—25 stitches.

Row 5: Purl across.

Row 6: *K3, M1; repeat from the * across, ending with k1—33 stitches.

Rows 7-11: Beginning with a purl (WS) row, work even in Stockinette Stitch.

Row 12 (RS): *K2, k2tog; repeat from the * across, ending with k1—25 stitches.

Row 13: Purl across.

Row 14: *K1, k2tog; repeat from the * across, ending with k1—17 stitches.

Row 15: Purl across.

Row 16: *K2tog; repeat from the * across, ending with k1—9 stitches.

Row 17: *P2tog (page 145), p1; repeat from the * around—6 stitches.

FIRST SEGMENT
Row 1 (RS): Change to B, *k1, M1; repeat from the * across, ending with k1—11 stitches.

Row 2: Purl across.

Row 3: *K2, M1; repeat from the * across, ending with k1—16 stitches.

Row 4: Purl across.

Row 5: *K3, M1; repeat from the * across, ending with k1—21 stitches.

Rows 6-10: Beginning with a purl row, work Stockinette Stitch.

Row 11: *K2, k2tog; repeat from the * across, ending with k1—16 stitches.

Row 12: Purl across.

Row 13: *K1, k2tog; repeat from the * across, ending with k1—11 stitches.

Row 14: Purl across.

Row 15: *K2tog; repeat from the * across, ending with k1—6 stitches.

Row 16: Purl across.

SECOND SEGMENT
Row 1 (RS): Change to C and work same as first segment.

THIRD SEGMENT
Row 1 (RS): Change to D and work same as first segment.

FOURTH SEGMENT
Row 1 (RS): Change to E and work same as first segment.

Finishing

ANTENNA (MAKE 2)

With RS facing and A, use a double-pointed needle to pick up and knit 1 stitch at the rear top of the head.

Row 1 (RS): Knit into the front, back, and front of the stitch—3 stitches. *Do not turn. Slide to the beginning of the row* (page 150).

Rows 2–8: Work I-cord.

Rows 9–14: Change to D and work I-cord. *Do not turn. Slide.*

Row 15: K3tog—1 stitch remains.

Fasten off, leaving a 6 in/15 cm tail.

Use yarn tail to coil the last 7 rows and secure to the first row of D for the top of the antenna.

Using black embroidery floss or yarn, embroider eyes as seen in photo.

Stuffing as you go, sew the seam.

Darn in all remaining yarn tails.

Preppy Socks

#InstaKnitsForBaby_PreppySocks

TIME TO KNIT 2½ to 3½ hours, depending on the size

SIZES

0–3 Months (3–6 Months,
6–12 Months, 12–18 Months).
Instructions are for the smallest
size with changes for larger sizes
in parentheses as necessary.

FINISHED MEASUREMENTS

Foot Circumference: 3¼ (4, 4, 5) in/
8.5 (10, 10, 13) cm
Foot Length: 3 (3½, 4, 4½) in/7.5 (9, 10, 11.5) cm

MATERIALS

- Berroco *Comfort* (#4 medium weight; 50%
  super fine nylon/50% super fine acrylic;
  each approximately 3½ oz/100 g and
  210 yd/193 m), 1 skein each of Raspberry
  Sorbet #9728 (A) and Robin's Egg #9714
  (B)
- Double-pointed knitting needles, US sizes
  6 and 7 (4 and 4.5 mm) or size needed to
  obtain gauge
- 2 Stitch markers
- 1 Stitch holder

GAUGE

In Stockinette Stitch and with the larger
needles, 20 stitches and 26 rounds = 4 in/
10 cm, blocked.

To save time, take time to check gauge.

Stockinette Stitch Worked in the Round
Pattern Round (RS): Knit.

Repeat the Pattern Round for the pattern.

NOTE: *This design is worked in the round
from the top down.*

SOCK (MAKE 2)

CUFF

With A, cast on 16 (20, 20, 24) stitches onto a smaller double-pointed needle.

Divide the stitches evenly between 4 of the smaller double-pointed needles. Place a marker for the beginning of the round and join for circular knitting, being careful not to twist the stitches.

Round 1 (RS): *K1-tbl, p1; repeat from the * around.

Repeat the last round until the piece measures approximately 1 in/2.5 cm from the beginning.

LEG

Change to the larger double-pointed needles, B, and Stockinette Stitch Worked in the Round and work even until the piece measures approximately 3½ in/9 cm from the beginning.

K8 (10, 10, 12) stitches and slip them onto a holder.

HEEL

Begin Short Rows

Row 1 (RS): Change to A and k7 (9, 9, 11), w&t (page 156).

Row 2: P6 (8, 8, 10), w&t.

Row 3: Knit across to 1 stitch before the wrapped stitch, w&t.

Row 4: Purl across to 1 stitch before the wrapped stitch, w&t.

Rows 5–8: Repeat Rows 3 and 4 until only 2 stitches remain between wrapped stitches, ending after WS row.

Second Half of Heel

Row 1 (RS): Knit across to the first wrapped stitch, knit the wrapped stitch along with its wrap, turn.

Row 2: Slip the first stitch purlwise with the yarn in front, purl across to the next wrapped stitch, purl the wrapped stitch along with its wrap, turn.

Repeat the last 2 rows until all wraps have been picked up, ending after a WS row resolving the last wrapped stitch and its wrap.

FOOT

Change to B, knit across the 8 (10, 10, 12) heel stitches, and knit across the 8 (10, 10, 12) stitches from the holder—16 (20, 20, 24) stitches.

Continue even in Stockinette Stitch Worked in the Round until the piece measures approximately 1 (1½, 2, 2½) in/2.5 (4, 5, 6.5) cm from the back of the heel. Place a marker in the middle of the round.

Decrease for the Toe

Next Round: With A, k1, ssk (page 153), knit across to 3 stitches before the middle marker, k2tog, k1, slip the marker, k1, ssk, knit across to 3 stitches before the next marker, k2tog, k1.

Next Round: Knit around.

Repeat the last 2 rounds until you have 8 (8, 8, 12) stitches remaining.

Next Round: *K2tog; repeat from the * around—4 (4, 4, 6) stitches remain.

Cut the yarn, leaving a 6 in/15 cm tail for sewing.

Thread the tail through the remaining 4 (4, 4, 6) stitches and pull tight.

Finishing
Darn in all yarn tails.

Block piece to measurements.

Just Ducky

#InstaKnitsForBaby_JustDucky

SIZE
One size

FINISHED MEASUREMENTS
12 × 12 in/30.5 × 30.5 cm

MATERIALS
- Berroco *Vintage Chunky* (#5 bulky weight; 52% acrylic/40% wool/8% nylon; each approximately 3½ oz/100 g and 136 yd/125 m), 1 hank each of Banane #6122 (A) and Guava #61193 (B)
- Circular knitting needles, US size 10 (6 mm) or size needed to obtain gauge
- Double-pointed knitting needle, US size 10 (6 mm) or size needed to obtain gauge
- 1 Yd/1 m of black yarn or embroidery floss
- Fiberfill stuffing

GAUGE
In Garter Stitch, 15 stitches and 30 rows = 4 in/10 cm, blocked.

To save time, take time to check gauge.

> **NOTES:**
> - *This blanket is worked on the diagonal.*
> - *The circular knitting needle is used to accommodate the large number of stitches. Do not join at the end of rows; instead, work back and forth in rows.*

Garter Stitch (Over Any Number of Stitches)
Row 1 (RS): Knit across.

Row 2: Knit across.

Repeat Rows 1 and 2 for the pattern.

I-Cord (Over 5 Stitches)
Pattern Row (RS): Knit across. *Do not turn. Slide to the beginning of the row (page 150).*

Repeat the Pattern Row.

BLANKET

With A, cast on 4 stitches.

Begin Increasing
Row 1 (RS): K2, yarn over, k2—5 stitches.

Row 2: K2, yarn over, k3—6 stitches.

Row 3: K2, yarn over, k2tog, yarn over, k2—7 stitches.

Row 4: K2, yarn over, k2tog, yarn over, k3—8 stitches.

Rows 5–56: K2, yarn over, k2tog, yarn over, knit across the rest of the row. Each row will add 1 stitch—60 stitches at the end of Row 56.

Begin Decreasing
Row 57 (RS): K1, [k2tog, yarn over] twice, k2tog, knit across 53 stitches to end the row—59 stitches remain.

Rows 58–100: K1, [k2tog, yarn over] twice, k2tog, knit across the rest of the row. Each row will decrease by 1 stitch; there will be 16 stitches remaining at the end of Row 100.

HEAD
Row 1 (WS): Use the knit-on cast-on technique and A to cast on 16 stitches then knit them; knit across the 16 stitches remaining at the end of Row 100—32 stitches.

Rows 2–11: Knit across.

Row 12: K2, [k2tog, k1] 10 times—22 stitches remain.

Row 13: Knit across.

Row 14: K1, [k2tog, k1] 7 times—15 stitches remain.

Row 15: Knit across.

Row 16: [K2tog, k1] 5 times—10 stitches remain.

Do not bind off.

Close the Top of Head
Slip the first 5 stitches onto a double-pointed knitting needle and hold in front of the main needle with the wrong sides facing each other.

Use another double-pointed knitting needle to work a three needle bind-off (page 155).

Fasten off.

BEAK (MAKE 1)
With B, cast on 8 stitches.

Rows 1–6: Knit across.

Row 7: K1, k2tog, k2, k2tog, k1—6 stitches.

Row 8: Knit across.

Row 9: K1, M1 (page 144), k4, M1, k1—8 stitches.

Rows 10–14: Knit across.

Knit as you bind off.

LEGS (MAKE 2)

With B, cast on 5 stitches.

Work I-cord until the cord measures approximately 3¼ in/8.5 cm.

Increase for Foot

Next Row: [K1, M1] 4 times, k1—9 stitches. Turn.

Next Row: K2, [M1, k1] 5 times, M1, k2—15 stitches.

Next Row: Knit across.

Make Toes

First Toe: K1, s2kp2 (page 152), k1, turn, leaving rest of row unworked; k1, p1, k1, turn; s2kp2, fasten off.

Second Toe: Reattach yarn and k5, turn, leaving rest of row unworked; k2, p1, k2, turn; k1, s2kp2, k1, turn; k1, p1, k1, turn; s2kp2, fasten off.

Third Toe: Same as second toe.

Finishing

Using the black yarn or embroidery floss, embroider the eyes and eyebrows as shown in the photograph.

Sew the center row of the beak onto the RS of the head, leaving the cast-on and bound-off edges unsewn.

Sew on the legs as shown in the photograph.

Stuff the head. Sew the back lower and side head seams.

Darn in all remaining yarn tails.

Elfin Booties

#InstaKnitsForBaby_ElfinBooties

TIME TO KNIT 3½ to 4 hours, depending on the size

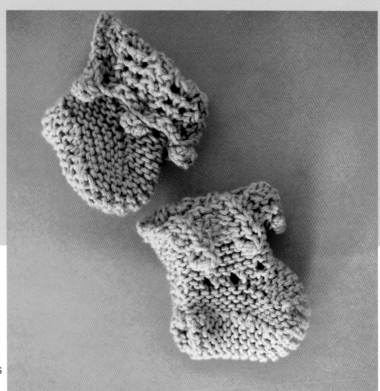

SIZES

0–3 Months (3–6 Months, 6–12 Months). Instructions are for the smallest size with changes for other sizes noted in parentheses as necessary.

FINISHED MEASUREMENTS

Length: 3 (3½, 3¾) in/7.5 (9, 9.5) cm

MATERIALS

- Lion Brand *24/7 Cotton* (#4 medium weight; 100% mercerized cotton; each approximately 3½ oz/100 g and 186 yd/ 170 m), 1 ball of Succulent #116
- Knitting needles, US size 5 (3.75 mm) or size needed to obtain gauge
- Knitting needles, US size 6 (4 mm)
- Optional: Approximately 18 in/45.5 cm of ribbon, ¼ in/0.5 cm wide

GAUGE

In Garter Stitch with the smaller needles, 20 stitches and 40 rows = 4 in/10 cm, blocked.

To save time, take time to check gauge.

Wave Pattern (Multiple of 6 + 1 Stitches)

Row 1 (RS): *K3, Bobble (page 132), k2; repeat from the * across, ending with k1.

Row 2: K3, *p1, k5; repeat from the * across, ending with p1, k3.

Row 3: *K1, yarn over, k1, s2kp2 (page 152), k1, yarn over; repeat from the * across, ending with k1.

Row 4: As Row 2.

Repeat Rows 3 and 4 for the pattern.

Garter Stitch

Row 1 (RS): Knit across.

Pattern Row: As Row 1.

BOOTIE (MAKE 2)

With the larger needles, cast on 25 (31, 31) stitches.

Begin the Wave Pattern. Work Rows 1–4 once, then repeat Rows 3 and 4 until the piece measures approximately 1½ in/4 cm from the beginning.

Change to the smaller needles, begin Garter Stitch, decrease 2 (6, 4) stitches evenly spaced along the first row—23 (25, 27) stitches remain.

Continue even in Garter Stitch until the piece measures approximately 3 in/7.5 cm from the beginning, ending after WS row, increase (increase, decrease) 2 (0, 2) stitches evenly spaced across the last row—25 stitches.

Next Row (Eyelet Row): K1, *k2tog, yarn over, k1; repeat from the * across.

Next Row: Knit across, decrease (decrease, increase) 2 (0, 2) stitches evenly across the row—23 (25, 27) stitches.

Shape Toe

Next Row (RS): K15 (17, 18), turn, leaving the rest of the row unworked.

Next Row: Slip the first stitch with the yarn in back, k6 (8, 8), turn, leaving the rest of the row unworked.

Repeat the last row 6 (10, 12) more times.

Side of Toe

Next Row (WS): Using the tip of the left needle, pick up and knit 4 (6, 7) stitches along the side of the 8 (12, 14) toe rows, then knit 8 (8, 9) stitches, turn.

Next Row: K19 (23, 25), use the tip of the left needle to pick up and knit 4 (6, 7) stitches along t12 (12.5, 14) toe rows, then k8 (8, 9) to end the row—31 (37, 41) stitches.

Knit 5 rows of Garter Stitch.

Sole

Next Row (RS): K18 (22, 24), k2tog, turn, leaving the rest of the row unworked.

Next Row: K6 (8, 8), k2tog, turn, leaving the rest of the row unworked.

Repeat the last row until there are 7 (9, 9) stitches remaining.

Bind off, leaving a 12 in/30.5 cm tail.

Finishing

Block to finished measurements.

Use the yarn tail to seam the back of the bootie, pinching the back of the sole together as necessary.

Optional: Thread ribbon through eyelets at the ankle.

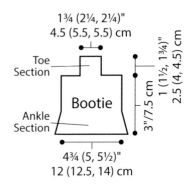

1¾ (2¼, 2¼)"
4.5 (5.5, 5.5) cm

Toe Section

Bootie

Ankle Section

3"/7.5 cm

1 (1½, 1¾)"
2.5 (4, 4.5) cm

4¾ (5, 5½)"
12 (12.5, 14) cm

Lamb Hat

#InstaKnitsForBaby_LambHat

TIME TO KNIT 1½ to 2 hours, depending on the size

SIZES

0–6 Months (6–9 Months,
9–12 Months, 12–24 Months).
Instructions are for the smallest
size with changes for larger sizes
in parentheses as necessary.

FINISHED MEASUREMENTS

Circumference: 12 (14, 16, 18) in/30.5 (35.5,
40.5, 45.5) cm
Height: 6½ (7, 7½, 7½) in/16.5 (18, 19, 19) cm

MATERIALS

- Berroco *Deluxe Bulky Superwash* (#5
  bulky weight; 100% superwash wool; each
  approximately 3½ oz/100 g and 106 yd/97
  m), 1 ball each of Pulp #928 (A) and Petit
  Pink #923 (B)
- Circular knitting needle, US size 10½ (6.5
  mm) or size needed to obtain gauge, 16
  in/40 cm length
- Double-pointed knitting needles, US size
  10½ (6.5 mm) or size needed to obtain
  gauge
- Stitch marker

GAUGE

In Stockinette Stitch, 12 stitches and 16
rounds = 4 in/10 cm, blocked.

To save time, take time to check gauge.

Seed Stitch Worked in the Round
(Over an Even Number of Stitches)

Round 1 (RS): *K1, p1; repeat from the *
around.

Round 2: *P1, k1; repeat from the * around.

Repeat Rounds 1 and 2 for the pattern.

Stockinette Stitch Worked in the Round
Pattern Round (RS): Knit around.

NOTES:
- *This design is knitted in the round from
  the bottom up.*
- *Change to the double-pointed needles
  when necessary to accommodate the
  smaller number of stitches.*

HAT

BODY
With A, cast on 36 (42, 48, 54) stitches onto the circular needle. Place a marker for the beginning of the round and join for circular knitting, being careful not to twist the stitches.

Begin Seed Stitch Worked in the Round, and work even until the piece measures approximately 1½ in/4 cm from the beginning.

Begin Stockinette Stitch Worked in the Round and work even until the piece measures approximately 5¼ (5¾, 6¼, 6¼) in/13.5 (14.5, 16, 16) cm from the beginning.

CROWN
Crown Round 1: *Ssk (page 153), k4; repeat from the * around—30 (35, 40, 45) stitches remain.

Crown Round 2: *Ssk, k3; repeat from the * around—24 (28, 32, 36) stitches remain.

Crown Round 3: *Ssk, k2; repeat from the * around—18 (21, 24, 27) stitches remain.

Crown Round 4: *Ssk, k1; repeat from the * around—12 (14, 16, 18) stitches remain.

Crown Round 5: *Ssk; repeat from the * around—6 (7, 8, 9) stitches remain.

Thread the tail through the remaining 6 (7, 8, 9) stitches and pull tight.

Finishing
Block to finished measurements.

EAR (MAKE 2)
With A, cast on 10 stitches.

Row 1: Kf&b (page 141), k8, kf&b—12 stitches.

Row 2: Kf&b, k10, kf&b—14 stitches.

Rows 3–6: Knit across.

Rows 7 and 8: Change to B and knit across.

Row 9: K2tog, k10, k2tog—12 stitches.

Row 10: K2tog, k8, k2tog—10 stitches.

Bind off.

Fold each ear in half and seam the side edges. Seam the beginning and end of the wide edge together to form the base of each ear.

Sew ears onto the sides of hat as seen in the photo.

Nordic Earflap Hat

#InstaKnitsForBaby_NordicEarflapHat

TIME TO KNIT 3½ to 4 hours, depending on the size

SIZES

0–3 Months (3–6 Months, 6–24 Months). Instructions are for the smallest size with changes for larger sizes in parentheses as necessary.

FINISHED MEASUREMENTS

Circumference: 12 (14½, 17) in/30.5 (37, 43) cm
Height: 6 (6½, 7) in/15 (16.5, 18) cm

MATERIALS

- Berroco *Comfort Worsted* (#4 medium weight; 50% nylon/50% acrylic; each approximately 3½ oz/100 g and 210 yd/193 m), 1 skein each of #Turquoise 9733 (A), Pearl #9702 (B), Buttercup #9712 (C), and Robin's Egg #9714 (D)
- Circular knitting needle, US size 7 (4.5 mm) or size needed to obtain gauge, 16 in/40 cm in length
- Double-pointed knitting needles, US size 7 (4.5 mm) or size needed to obtain gauge
- Stitch marker

GAUGE

In the Nordic-Style Pattern, 20 stitches and 24 rounds = 4 in/10 cm, blocked.

To save time, take time to check gauge.

NOTES:
- *This design is made in the round from the bottom up.*
- *Change to the double-pointed needles when necessary to accommodate the smaller number of stitches.*

Garter Stitch Worked in the Round

Round 1: Knit around.

Round 2: Purl around.

Repeat Rounds 1 and 2 for the pattern.

HAT

BODY

With A, cast on 53 (64, 76) stitches onto the circular needle. Place a marker for the beginning of the round, and join for circular knitting, being careful not to twist the stitches.

Begin Garter Stitch Worked in the Round, and work even for 6 rounds; use the M1 technique (page 144) to increase 7 (8, 8) stitches evenly spaced along the last round—60 (72, 84) stitches.

Begin the Nordic-Style Pattern and work even until the piece measures approximately 5½ (6, 6½) in/14 (15, 16.5) cm from the beginning, ending after a round worked with solid A.

CROWN

Crown Round 1: Continuing with A for the rest of the crown, *ssk (page 153), k4; repeat from the * around—50 (60, 70) stitches remain.

Crown Round 2: *Ssk, k3; repeat from the * around—40 (48, 56) stitches remain.

Crown Round 3: *Ssk, k2; repeat from the * around—30 (36, 42) stitches remain.

Crown Round 4: *Ssk, k1; repeat from the * around—20 (24, 28) stitches remain.

Crown Round 5: *Ssk; repeat from the * around—10 (12, 14) stitches remain.

Cut the yarn, leaving a 6 in/15 cm tail for sewing.

Thread the tail through the remaining 10 (12, 14) stitches and pull tight.

EARFLAPS
With RS facing and A, count 8 (10, 12) stitches from the center back of the hat and pick up and knit 10 (12, 14) stitches working away from the back of the hat.

Knit 3 rows.

Change to D and knit 2 rows.

Next Row (Decrease Row): K2tog, knit across to the last 2 stitches, k2tog.

Next Row: Knit across.

Change to C and repeat the last 2 rows twice more—4 (6, 8) stitches remain.

Bind off.

Repeat for the second earflap.

Darn in all yarn tails.

Block to finished measurements.

Nordic-Style Pattern

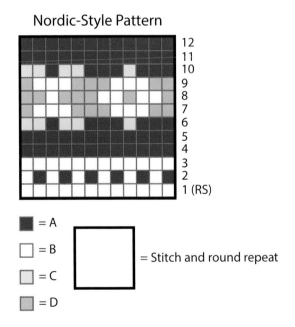

■ = A

□ = B

□ = C

■ = D

= Stitch and round repeat

Beach Ball

#InstaKnitsForBaby_BeachBall

TIME TO KNIT 2 hours

FINISHED MEASUREMENTS
Diameter: 5½ in/14 cm

MATERIALS
- Knitting Fever, Inc/Juniper Moon Farm *Nimbus* (#5 bulky weight; 96% Mako cotton/4% nylon; each approximately 3½ oz/100 g and 164 yd/128 m), 1 ball each of Honeydew #07 (A) and Alabaster #01 (B)
- Knitting needles, US size 9 (5.5 mm) or size needed to obtain gauge
- Fiberfill stuffing

GAUGE
In Garter Stitch, 15 stitches and 30 rows = 4 in/10 cm, blocked.

To save time, take time to check gauge.

NOTE: *This design is made sideways using short rows.*

BALL

With A, cast on 24 stitches.

Row 1 (RS): Knit across.

Row 2: K18, turn, leaving the rest of the row unworked.

Row 3: K16, turn, leaving the rest of the row unworked.

Row 4: K18, turn, leaving the rest of the row unworked.

Rows 5–8: As Rows 3 and 4.

Rows 9–16: With B, as Rows 1–8.

Rows 17–24: With A, as Rows 1–8.

Rows 25–32: With B, as Rows 1–8.

Rows 33–40: With A, as Rows 1–8.

Rows 41–48: With B, as Rows 1–8.

Rows 49–56: With A, as Rows 1–8.

Rows 57–64: With B, as Rows 1–8.

Rows 65–72: With A, as Rows 1–8.

Rows 73–80: With B, as Rows 1–8.

Rows 81–88: With A, as Rows 1–8.

Rows 89–96: With B, as Rows 1–8.

Bind off.

Finishing

Stuffing as you go, sew the side seam.

Thread yarn through the sides of rows on one side and pull tight.

Repeat along the other side.

Darn in all yarn tails.

Bonny Bib

#InstaKnitsForBaby_BonnyBib

TIME TO KNIT 2 hours

SIZES
One size

FINISHED MEASUREMENTS
Width: 11 in/28 cm
Height: 9½ in/24 cm

MATERIALS
- Skacel/HiKoo *Simpliworsted* (#4 medium weight; 55% superwash merino wool/28% acrylic/17% nylon; each approximately 3½ oz/100 g and 140 yd/128 m), 1 hank of Blooming Rose #022
- Knitting needles, US size 10 (6 mm) or size needed to obtain gauge
- ½ yd/0.5 m of ribbon, 1 in/2.5 cm wide

GAUGE
In Garter Stitch, 14 stitches and 28 rows = 4 in/10 cm, blocked.

To save time, take time to check gauge.

NOTE: *This design is made sideways using short rows.*

BIB

Cast on 17 stitches.

Row 1 (RS): K12, yarn over, ssk (page 153), k3.

Row 2: K2, yarn over, k1, p2, yarn over, p2tog, k9, turn, leaving the rest of the row unworked.

Row 3: K11, yarn over, ssk, k2, yarn over, k2.

Row 4: K3, yarn over, k2, p2, yarn over, p2tog, k8, turn, leaving the rest of the row unworked.

Row 5: K10, yarn over, ssk, k3, yarn over, k3.

Row 6: Bind off the first 4 stitches, knit the next 2 stitches, p2, yarn over, p2tog, k7, turn, leaving the rest of the row unworked.

Row 7: K9, yarn over, ssk, k3.

Row 8: K2, yarn over, k1, p2, yarn over, p2tog, k6, turn, leaving the rest of the row unworked.

Row 9: K8, yarn over, ssk, k2, yarn over, k2.

Row 10: K3, yarn over, k2, p2, yarn over, p2tog, k5, turn, leaving the rest of the row unworked.

Row 11: K7, yarn over, ssk, k3, yarn over, k3.

Row 12: Bind off the first 4 stitches, knit the next 2 stitches, p2, yarn over, p2tog, k4, turn, leaving the rest of the row unworked.

Row 13: K6, yarn over, ssk, k3.

Row 14: K2, yarn over, k1, p2, yarn over, p2tog, k3, turn, leaving the rest of the row unworked.

Row 15: K5, yarn over, ssk, k2, yarn over, k2.

Row 16: K3, yarn over, k2, p2, yarn over, p2tog, k2, turn, leaving the rest of the row unworked.

Row 17: K4, yarn over, ssk, k3, yarn over, k3.

Row 18: Bind off the first 4 stitches, k2, p2, yarn over, p2tog, k10, turn.

Repeat Rows 1–18 5 *more* times.

Bind off.

Finishing
Darn in all yarn tails.

Block piece to measurements.

Sew on ribbon for ties as shown in the photograph.

Clownfish Teether

#InstaKnitsForBaby_ClownfishTeether

TIME TO KNIT 3 hours

SIZE
One Size

FINISHED MEASUREMENTS
Width: 2½ in/6.5 cm
Length: 6½ in/16.5 cm, excluding ring

MATERIALS
- Berroco *Vintage* (#4 medium weight; 52% acrylic/40% wool/8% nylon; each approximately 3½ oz/100 g and 218 yd/200 m), 1 ball each of Watermelon #5126 (A), Cast Iron #5145 (B), and Banane [*sic*] #5122 (C)
- Knitting needles, US size 7 (4.5 mm) or size needed to obtain gauge
- Fiberfill stuffing
- 1 Wood teether ring, 2¾ in/7 cm diameter

GAUGE
In Stockinette Stitch, 20 stitches and 27 rows = 4 in/10 cm, blocked.

To save time, take time to check gauge.

Stockinette Stitch (Over Any Number of Stitches)
Row 1 (RS): Knit across.

Row 2: Purl across.

Repeat Rows 1 and 2 for the pattern.

FISH

With A, cast on 3 stitches.

Row 1 (RS): Knit across.

Row 2: P1, M1 purlwise (page 145), p1, M1 purlwise, p1—5 stitches.

Row 3: K2, M1 (page 144), k1, M1, k2—7 stitches.

Row 4: Purl across.

Row 5: K2, M1, k3, M1, k2—9 stitches.

Row 6: Purl across.

Row 7: Change to B, k2, M1, k5, M1, k2—11 stitches.

Row 8: Change to C, purl across.

Row 9: K2, M1, k7, M1, k2—13 stitches.

Rows 10-12: Beginning with a purl row, work Stockinette Stitch.

Row 13: K2, M1, k9, M1, k2—15 stitches.

Row 14: Change to B, purl across.

Rows 15 and 16: Change to A and beginning with a knit row, work Stockinette Stitch.

Row 17: K2, M1, k11, M1, k2—17 stitches.

Rows 18-20: Beginning with a purl row, work Stockinette Stitch.

Row 21: Change to B, knit across.

Row 22: Change to C, purl across.

Rows 23-27: Beginning with a knit row, work Stockinette Stitch.

Row 28: Change to B, purl across.

Row 29: Change to A, k1, ssk (page 153), k11, k2tog, k1—15 stitches.

Rows 30-32: Beginning with a purl row, work Stockinette Stitch.

Row 33: K1, ssk, k9, k2tog, k1—13 stitches.

Row 34: Purl across.

Row 35: Change to B, k1, ssk, k7, k2tog, k1—11 stitches.

Row 36: Change to C, purl across.

Row 37: K1, ssk, k5, k2tog, k1—9 stitches.

Row 38: Purl across.

Row 39: K1, ssk, k3, k2tog, k1—7 stitches.

Row 40: Purl across.

Row 41: K1, ssk, k1, k2tog, k1—5 stitches.

Row 42: Change to B, purl across.

Row 43: Change to A, knit across.

Row 44: P2, M1 purlwise, p1, M1 purlwise, p2—7 stitches.

Row 45: K2, M1, k3, M1, k2—9 stitches.

Row 46: P2, M1 purlwise, p5, M1 purlwise, p2—11 stitches.

Row 47: K2, M1, k7, M1, k2—13 stitches.

Row 48: P2, M1 purlwise, p9, M1 purlwise, p2—15 stitches.

Rows 49–52: Beginning with a knit row, work Stockinette Stitch.

Row 53: K1, ssk, k9, k2tog, k1—13 stitches.

Row 54: P1, p2tog, p7, ssp (page 154), p1—11 stitches.

Row 55: K1, ssk, k5, k2tog, k1—9 stitches.

Row 56: P1, p2tog, p3, ssp, p1—7 stitches.

Row 57: K1, ssk, k1, k2tog, k1—5 stitches.

Row 58: Purl across.

Row 59: Change to B, k2, M1, k1, M1, k2—7 stitches.

Row 60: Change to C, purl across.

Row 61: K2, M1, k3, M1, k2—9 stitches.

Row 62: Purl across.

Row 63: K2, M1, k5, M1, k2—11 stitches.

Row 64: Purl across.

Row 65: K2, M1, k7, M1, k2—13 stitches.

Row 66: Change to B, purl across.

Row 67: Change to A, K2, M1, k9, M1, k2—15 stitches.

Rows 68–70: Beginning with a purl row, work Stockinette Stitch.

Row 71: K2, M1, k11, M1, k2—17 stitches.

Row 72: Purl across.

Row 73: Change to B, knit across.

Rows 74–79: Change to C and beginning with a purl row, work Stockinette Stitch.

Row 80: Change to B, purl across.

Rows 81 and 82: Change to A and beginning with a knit row, work Stockinette Stitch.

Row 83: K1, ssk, k11, k2tog, k1—15 stitches.

Rows 84–86: Beginning with a purl row, work Stockinette Stitch.

Row 87: Change to B, k1, ssk, k9, k2tog, k1—13 stitches.

Rows 88–90: Change to C and beginning with a purl row, work Stockinette Stitch.

Row 91: K1, ssk, k7, k2tog, k1—11 stitches.

Row 92: Purl across.

Row 93: K1, ssk, k5, k2tog, k1—9 stitches.

Row 94: Change to B, purl across.

Row 95: Change to A, k1, ssk, k3, k2tog, k1—7 stitches.

Row 96: Purl across.

Row 97: K1, ssk, k1, k2tog, k1—5 stitches.

Row 98: P2tog, p1, ssp (page 154)—3 stitches.

Row 99: Knit across.

Bind off.

Finishing

Thread the fish through the ring, then fold in half.

Stuffing with fiberfill as you go, sew the sides of the fish together.

Sew a straight line at the narrowest part of the tail to prevent the stuffing from getting into the tail section.

With B, embroider eyes and smile on both sides of fish.

Baseball Cap

#InstaKnitsForBaby_BaseballCap

TIME TO KNIT 3 to 5 hours, depending on the size

SIZES

0–6 Months (6–12 Months, 12–24 Months). Instructions are for the smallest size with changes for larger sizes in parentheses as necessary.

FINISHED MEASUREMENTS

Circumference: 12 (15, 17) in/30.5 (38, 43) cm
Height: 7 (8, 9) in/18 (20.5, 23) cm

MATERIALS

- Lion Brand *Wool Ease Thick and Quick* (#6 super bulky weight; 80% acrylic/20% wool; each approximately 5 oz/140 g and 87 yd/80 m), 1 ball of Carousel #619
- Circular knitting needle, US size 13 (9 mm) or size needed to obtain gauge, 16 in/40 cm in length
- Double-pointed knitting needles, US size 13 (9 mm) or size needed to obtain gauge
- Stitch marker
- One sheet of plastic canvas

GAUGE

In Stockinette Stitch, 9 stitches and 12 rounds = 4 in/10 cm, blocked.

To save time, take time to check gauge.

Garter Stitch Worked in the Round

Round 1: Knit.

Round 2: Purl.

Repeat Rounds 1 and 2 for the pattern.

Stockinette Stitch Worked in the Round

Pattern Round (RS): Knit.

Repeat the Pattern Round for the pattern.

Garter Stitch Worked Flat

Pattern Row: Knit.

NOTES:
- *This design is made in the round from the bottom up.*
- *Change to the double-pointed needles when necessary to accommodate the smaller number of stitches.*

HAT

BODY

Cast on 24 (29, 32) stitches onto the circular needle. Place a marker for the beginning of the round, and join for circular knitting, being careful not to twist the stitches.

Begin Garter Stitch Worked in the Round, and work even until the piece measures approximately 1 in/2.5 cm from the beginning; use the M1 technique (page 144) to increase 4 (5, 6) stitches evenly spaced across the last round—28 (34, 38) stitches.

Begin Stockinette Stitch Worked in the Round and work even until the piece measures approximately 3½ (4½, 5½) in/9 (11.5, 14) cm from the beginning; use the k2tog technique (page 143) to decrease 4 (2, 6) stitches evenly across the last round—24 (32, 32) stitches remain.

Decrease for the Crown

Decrease Round 1: *Ssk (page 153), k6; repeat from the * around—21 (28, 28) stitches remain.

Decrease Round 2: *Ssk, k5; repeat from the * around—18 (24, 24) stitches remain.

Decrease Round 3: *Ssk, k4; repeat from the * around—15 (20, 20) stitches remain.

Decrease Round 4: *Ssk, k3; repeat from the * around—12 (16, 16) stitches remain.

Decrease Round 5: *Ssk, k2; repeat from the * around—9 (12, 12) stitches remain.

Decrease Round 6: *Sssk (page 154); repeat from the * around—3 (4, 4) stitches remain.

Cut the yarn, leaving a 6 in/15 cm tail for sewing.

Thread the tail through the remaining 3 (4, 4) stitches and pull tight.

VISOR

With RS facing and *working through the back loops* of the cast-on edge, pick up and knit 12 (14, 16) stitches.

Begin Garter Stitch Worked Flat and use the k2tog technique to decrease 1 stitch each side every 4 rows twice—8 (10, 12) stitches remain.

Bind off.

Visor Facing

Cast on 12 (14, 16) stitches.

Complete same as for Visor.

Finishing

Cut plastic canvas to fit the Visor Facing.

Sandwich the piece of plastic canvas between the Visor and the Visor Facing, and whipstitch together.

Happy Hippo Rattle

#InstaKnitsForBaby_HappyHippoRattle

TIME TO KNIT 3 hours

FINISHED MEASUREMENTS

Height: 6½ in/16.5 cm
Width: 3 in/7.5 cm

MATERIALS

- Berroco *Comfort Chunky* (#5 bulky weight; 50% nylon/50% acrylic; each approximately 3½ oz/100 g and 150 yd/137 m), 1 ball each of Cornflower #5726 (A), Rosebud #5723 (B), and Ivory #5701 (C)
- Knitting needles, US size 10 (6 mm) or size needed to obtain gauge
- 1 yd/1 m of black yarn or embroidery floss
- Fiberfill stuffing
- Small container, approximately 1½ in/4 cm square, filled with beads and sealed tightly to prevent beads from escaping and presenting a choking hazard

GAUGE

In Stockinette Stitch, 18 stitches and 36 rows = 4 in/10 cm, blocked.

To save time, take time to check gauge.

Stockinette Stitch (Over Any Number of Stitches)

Row 1 (RS): Knit across.

Row 2: Purl across.

Repeat Rows 1 and 2 for the pattern.

RATTLE

HEAD

With A, cast on 10 stitches.

Row 1 (WS): Purl across.

Row 2: *K1, M1 (page 144); repeat from the * across, ending with k1—19 stitches.

Row 3: Purl across.

Row 4: *K2, M1; repeat from the * across, ending with k1—28 stitches.

Row 5: Purl across.

Row 6: *K3, M1; repeat from the * across, ending with k1—37 stitches.

Beginning with a purl (WS) row, work even in Stockinette Stitch until the piece measures approximately 2¼ in/5.5 cm from the beginning, ending after a purl row. Insert the small box with beads, and stuff the head with fiberfill as you continue to make the head.

Next Row (RS): *K2, k2tog; repeat from the * across, ending with k1—28 stitches.

Next Row: Purl across.

Next Row: *K1, k2tog; repeat from the * across, ending with k1—19 stitches.

Next Row: Purl across.

Next Row: *K2tog; repeat from the * across, ending with k1—10 stitches.

Cut the yarn, leaving a 6 in/15 cm tail for sewing.

Thread the tail through the remaining 10 stitches and pull tight.

SNOUT

With A, cast on 18 stitches.

Row 1 (WS): Purl across.

Row 2: K1, M1 (page 144), k7, M1, k2, M1, k7, M1, k1—22 stitches.

Rows 3-5: Beginning with a purl (WS) row, work 3 rows of Stockinette Stitch.

Row 6: K1, k2tog, k5, [k2tog] 3 times, k5, k2tog, k1—17 stitches.

Row 7: Purl across.

Row 8: Knit as you bind off.

Fold the snout in half and sew together 9 stitches to 9 stitches for the front of the snout.

Seam the side of the snout.

Stuff the snout and use the photograph as a guide as you sew the snout onto the lower portion of the head.

EAR (MAKE 2)

With A, cast on 3 stitches.

Row 1 (RS): Kf&b (page 141), k1, kf&b—5 stitches.

Rows 2-4: Knit across.

Row 5: Change to B, knit across.

Row 6: Knit across.

Row 7: K2tog, k1, k2tog—3 stitches.

Row 8: Knit as you bind off.

Fold each ear in half and seam the side edges. Seam the beginning and end of the wide edge together to form the base of the ears.

Using the photograph as a guide, sew ears onto the head.

Thread a 12 in/30.5 cm piece of A onto a yarn needle. Insert needle just below one ear, and going through the stuffing, bring it up just below the other ear. Repeat a few times to create slight indentations in the head below the ears, bringing the yarn through the stuffing each time so it is hidden.

Use black yarn or embroidery floss to embroider 2 straight nostrils on the snout and 2 eyes on the lower third of the head.

HANDLE

With the RS facing and A, pick up and knit 10 stitches in a circle on the lower quarter in the center back of the head.

Work Stockinette Stitch back and forth in rows as follows: *3 rows of A, 3 rows of C, 3 rows of B; repeat from the * once more.

Beginning with a knit (RS) row, work 5 rows of Stockinette Stitch.

Create Ridge

Next Row (WS): *Use the left-hand needle to pick up the purl bump of the next stitch 6 rows down, and purl this stitch together with the next stitch on the needle; repeat from the * across.

Decrease for Base

Next Row (RS): *Ssk, k3; repeat from the * across—8 stitches remain.

Next Row: *P2, ssp (page 154); repeat from the * across—6 stitches remain.

Next Row: [Sssk (page 154)] twice as you bind off.

Sew the seam of the handle, including the sides of the base, stuffing tightly as you go.

Pixie Hat

#InstaKnitsForBaby_PixieHat

TIME TO KNIT 3 to 5 hours, depending on the size

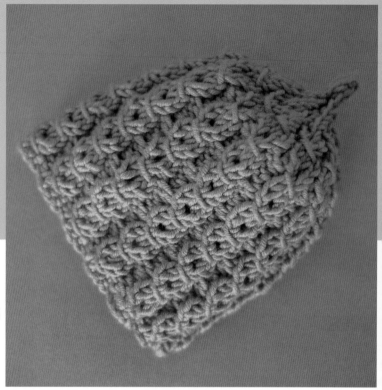

SIZES

0–6 Months (6–12 Months, 12–24 Months). Instructions are for the smallest size with changes for larger sizes in parentheses as necessary.

FINISHED MEASUREMENTS

Circumference: 12½ (15, 17½) in/32 (38, 44.5) cm
Height: 6½ (7½, 7½) in/16.5 (19, 19) cm

MATERIALS

- Skacel/HiKoo *Simpliworsted* (#4 medium weight; 55% superwash merino wool/28% acrylic/17% nylon; each approximately 3½ oz/100 g and 140 yd/128 m), 1 hank of Silver Blue #060
- Circular knitting needle, US size 10 (6 mm) or size needed to obtain gauge, 16 in/40 cm in length
- Double-pointed knitting needles, US size 10 (6 mm) or size needed to obtain gauge
- Stitch marker

GAUGE

In Petite Cable Pattern, 16 stitches and 21 rounds = 4 in/10 cm, blocked.

To save time, take time to check gauge.

Petite Cable Pattern (Multiple of 5 Stitches)

Rounds 1 and 2: *P1, k3, p1; repeat from the * around.

Round 3: *P1, slip the third stitch on the left needle over the first 2 stitches on the left needle (as if binding them off in the opposite direction), k1, yarn over, k1; p1; repeat from the * around.

Round 4: As Round 1.

Repeat Rounds 1–4 for the pattern.

NOTES:
- *This design is made in the round from the bottom up.*
- *Change to the double-pointed needles when necessary to accommodate the smaller number of stitches.*

HAT

BODY

Cast on 50 (60, 70) stitches onto the circular needle. Place a marker for the beginning of the round and join for circular knitting, being careful not to twist the stitches.

Begin the Petite Cable Pattern and work even until the piece measures approximately 5¼ (6¼, 6¼) in/13.5 (16, 16) cm from the beginning.

CROWN

Crown Round 1: *K2tog, k1, ssk; repeat from the * around—30 (36, 42) stitches remain.

Crown Round 2: *K2tog, k2, ssk; repeat from the * around—20 (24, 28) stitches remain.

Crown Round 3: *K2tog; repeat from the * around—10 (12, 14) stitches remain.

Crown Round 4: As Crown Round 3—5 (6, 7) stitches remain.

Crown Round 5: Knit.

Cut the yarn, leaving a 6 in/15 cm tail for sewing.

Thread the tail through the remaining 3 (4, 4) stitches and pull tight.

Finishing
Block to finished measurements.

Sprig Teether

#InstaKnitsForBaby_SprigTeether

FINISHED MEASUREMENTS

6½ in/16.5 cm wide, including leaves and teether ring

MATERIALS

- Cascade Yarn *220 Super-wash Merino* (#4 medium weight; 100% superwash merino wool; each approximately 3½ oz/100 g and 220 yd/200 m), 1 ball of Green Tea #17
- Knitting needles, US size 7 (4.5 mm) or size needed to obtain gauge
- 1 Wood teether ring, 2¾ in/7 cm diameter

GAUGE

In the pattern each leaf measures 1¾ in/4.5 cm wide and 3½ in/9 cm long, blocked.

I-Cord (Over 3 Stitches)

Pattern Row (RS): Knit across. *Do not turn. Slide to the beginning of the row* (page 150).

Repeat the Pattern Row.

TEETHER

FIRST LEAF

Cast on 11 stitches.

Row 1 (RS): Knit across.

Rows 2, 6, 10, and 14: K5, p1, k5.

Rows 3, 7, and 11: K1, M1 (page 144), k3, s2kp2 (page 152), k3, M1, k1—11 stitches.

Rows 4, 8, 12, 16, 20, and 24: Purl across.

Rows 5, 9, and 13: P5, k1, p5.

Row 15: K4, s2kp2, k4—9 stitches.

Row 17: P4, k1, p4.

Row 18: K4, p1, k4.

Row 19: K3, s2kp2, k3—7 stitches.

Row 21: P2, s2kp2, p2—5 stitches.

Row 22: K2, p1, k2.

Row 23: K1, s2kp2, k1—3 stitches.

Row 25: S2kp2.

Fasten off.

STEM AND SECOND LEAF

With the RS facing, pick up and knit 3 stitches in the middle of the cast-on edge of the first leaf.

Work I-cord until the cord measures approximately 4 in/10 cm.

Do not turn. Slide to the beginning of the row and s2kp2—1 stitch remains.

Next Row (RS): Use the knit-on technique (page 134) to cast on 5 stitches, then knit them and knit the 1 stitch remaining from the stem—6 stitches. Turn.

Next Row (WS): Use the knit-on technique to cast on 5 stitches, p1, k4—11 stitches.

Complete same as the first leaf, beginning with Row 3.

Finishing

Block to finished measurements.

Fold the piece in half, place on wooden ring and loop the stem over the two leaves. Sew a few stitches in the overhand loop to secure the leaves onto the ring.

Stuffed Froggy

#InstaKnitsForBaby_StuffedFroggy

TIME TO KNIT 3 hours

SIZES
One size

FINISHED MEASUREMENTS
3 × 9 in/7.5 × 23 cm, including
eyes and legs

MATERIALS
- Anzula *For Better or Worsted* (#4 medium
  weight; 80% superwash merino/10%
  cashmere/10% nylon; each approximately
  4 oz/114 g and 200 yd/182 m), 1 hank of
  Endora (A)
- ½ yd/0.5 m of white yarn or embroidery
  floss (doubled or tripled) (B)
- Double-pointed knitting needles, US size 8
  (5 mm) or size needed to obtain gauge
- 1 yd/1 m of black yarn or embroidery floss
- Fiberfill stuffing

GAUGE
In Garter Stitch with A, 18 stitches and 36
rows = 4 in/10 cm, blocked.

To save time, take time to check gauge.

Garter Stitch (Over Any Number of Stitches)
Row 1 (RS): Knit across.

Row 2: Knit across.

Repeat Rows 1 and 2 for the pattern.

I-Cord (Over 4 Stitches)
Pattern Row (RS): Knit across. *Do not turn.*
Slide to the beginning of the row (page 150).

Repeat the Pattern Row.

FROGGY

BODY

With A, cast on 30 stitches.

Begin Garter Stitch and work even until the piece measures approximately 4 in/10 cm from the beginning.

Slip 15 stitches to a double-pointed needle, and with WS facing each other, use a third double-pointed needle to work a three-needle bind-off (page 155).

EYE (MAKE 2)

With A, cast on 4 stitches.

Row 1 (RS): Kf&b (page 141), k2, kf&b—6 stitches.

Row 2: Knit across.

Row 3: Kf&b, k4, kf&b—8 stitches.

Row 4: Knit across.

Row 5: Change to B, and k2tog, k4, k2tog—6 stitches.

Row 6: Knit across.

Row 7: K2tog, k2, k2tog—4 stitches.

Bind off.

Fold each eye in half and seam the side edges. Seam the beginning and end of the wide edge together to form the base of each eye.

With the RS facing, refer to the photos, and use the black yarn or embroidery floss to add pupils to the bottom of the middle of each eye.

Referring to photos, sew eyes onto the three-needle bind-off on the body.

Stuff and sew the body side seam.

LEG (MAKE 2)

With the RS facing and A, pick up and knit 2 stitches on the front and 2 stitches on the back, close to the side edge of the frog—4 stitches.

Begin I-cord, and work even until the leg measures approximately 3¾ in/9.5 cm from the beginning. Do not bind off.

TOES

*Use the knit-on cast-on technique (page 134) to cast on 3 stitches.

Bind off 4 stitches.

Return the 1 stitch on the right needle back to the left needle.

Repeat from the * twice more.

Fasten off.

ARM (MAKE 2)

With the RS facing and A, pick up and knit 2 stitches on the front and 2 stitches on the back close to the side edge of the frog, approximately 1¼ in/3 cm down from the three-needle bind-off edge—4 stitches.

Complete same as the Legs and Toes.

Use the black yarn or embroidery floss to embroider a mouth as seen in the photo.

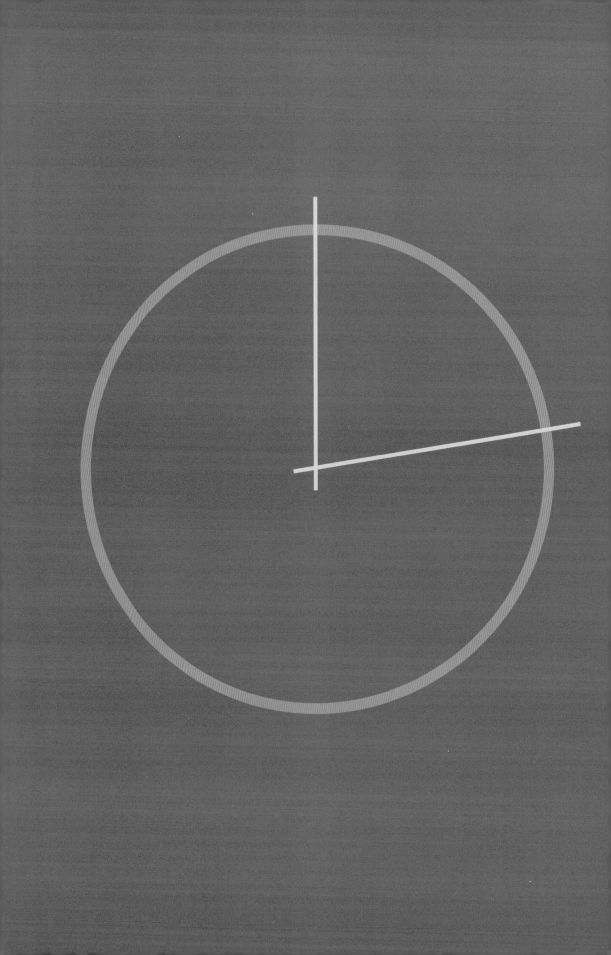

FIVE TO TEN HOURS

Spend just one weekend knitting in your
favorite armchair, and you can be the star
of your next baby shower (mom-to-be
notwithstanding, of course)! Just imagine
the smiles when she unwraps your adorable
Teddy or Koala Lovey!

Teddy Lovey

#InstaKnitsForBaby_TeddyLovey

SIZES
One size

FINISHED MEASUREMENTS
Height: 25¼ in/64 cm
Width: 23 in/58.5 cm

MATERIALS
- Berroco *Vintage Chunky* (#5 bulky weight; 52% acrylic/40% wool/8% nylon; each approximately 3½ oz/100 g and 136 yd/125 m), 1 hank each of Oats #6105 (A) and Mushroom #6104 (B)
- Circular knitting needle, US size 10 (6 mm) or size needed to obtain gauge, 24 in/60 cm
- Double-pointed knitting needles, US size 10 (6 mm) or size needed to obtain gauge
- 1 yd/1 m of black yarn or embroidery floss
- Fiberfill stuffing

GAUGE
In Garter Stitch, 15 stitches and 30 rows = 4 in/10 cm, blocked.

> **NOTES:**
> - *This blanket is worked on the diagonal.*
> - *The circular knitting needle is used to accommodate the large number of stitches. Do not join at the end of rows; instead, work back and forth in rows.*

Garter Stitch (Over Any Number of Stitches)
Row 1 (RS): Knit across.

Row 2: Knit across.

Repeat Rows 1 and 2 for the pattern.

LOVEY

BLANKET
With A, cast on 4 stitches.

Begin Increasing
Row 1 (RS): K2, yarn over, k2—5 stitches.

Row 2: K2, yarn over, k3—6 stitches.

Row 3: K2, yarn over, k2tog, yarn over, k2—7 stitches.

Row 4: K2, yarn over, k2tog, yarn over, k3—8 stitches.

Rows 5–84: K2, yarn over, k2tog, yarn over, knit across the rest of the row. Each row will add 1 stitch—88 stitches at the end of Row 84.

Begin Decreasing
Row 85 (RS): K1, [k2tog, yarn over] twice, k2tog, knit across 81 stitches to end the row—87 stitches remain.

Rows 86–150: K1, [k2tog, yarn over] twice, k2tog, knit across the rest of the row. Each row will decrease 1 stitch; there will be 22 stitches remaining at the end of Row 150. Do not bind off.

HEAD
Row 1 (WS): Use the knit-on cast-on technique and A to cast on 22 stitches then turn and knit them; knit across the 22 stitches remaining at the end of Row 150—44 stitches.

Rows 2–5: Knit across.

Row 6: K4, [k2tog, k3] 8 times—36 stitches remain.

Rows 7–9: Knit across.

Row 10: K1, [k2tog, k2] 8 times, k2tog, k1—27 stitches remain.

Rows 11–14: Knit across.

Row 15: K3, [k2tog, k2] 6 times—21 stitches remain.

Rows 16–18: Knit across.

Row 19: [K4, k2tog] 3 times, k3—18 stitches remain.

Do not bind off.

Close the Top of Head
Slip the first 9 stitches onto a double-pointed knitting needle and hold in front of the main needle with WS facing each other.

Use another double-pointed knitting needle to work a three-needle bind-off (page 155).

Fasten off.

SNOUT (MAKE 1)
With B, cast on 18 stitches.

Rows 1–4: Knit across.

Row 5 (RS): [K1, k2tog] 6 times—12 stitches remain.

Rows 6 and 7: Knit across.

Row 8: [K2tog] 6 times—6 stitches remain.

Row 9: Knit across.

Cut the yarn, leaving an 8 in/20.5 cm tail.

Thread the yarn tail through 6 remaining stitches and pull tight.

Use the yarn tail to seam the sides of the snout together.

EAR (MAKE 2)
With B, cast on 5 stitches.

Row 1 (RS): Kf&b (page 141), k3, kf&b—7 stitches.

Row 2: Knit across.

Row 3: Kf&b, k5, kf&b—9 stitches.

Row 4: Knit across.

Row 5: Kf&b, k7, kf&b—11 stitches.

Rows 6–8: Knit across.

Row 9: K2tog, k7, k2tog—9 stitches remain.

Row 10: Knit across.

Row 11: K2tog, k5, k2tog—7 stitches remain.

Row 12: Knit across.

Row 13: K2tog, k3, k2tog—5 stitches remain.

Row 14: Knit as you bind off.

Fold each ear in half and seam the side edges. Seam the beginning and end of the wide edge together to form the base of the ears.

Finishing
Using the black yarn or embroidery floss, embroider the nose and mouth onto the snout as shown in the photograph.

Sew the snout onto the RS of the head, stuffing as you go.

Use the black yarn or embroidery floss to embroider the eyes as shown in the photograph.

Sew on the ears as shown in the photograph.

Stuff the head. Sew the back lower and side head seam.

Darn in all remaining yarn tails.

Comfy Hoodie

#InstaKnitsForBaby_ComfyHoodie

TIME TO KNIT 10 hours

SIZES

6 Months (12 Months, 18 Months, 24 Months).
Instructions are for the smallest size, with
changes for other sizes noted in parentheses
as necessary.

FINISHED MEASUREMENTS

Chest: 21½ (24, 26½, 28) in/54.5 (61, 67.5, 71)
cm, buttoned
Length: 11 (12, 13, 14) in/28 (30.5, 33, 35.5) cm

MATERIALS

- Universal Yarn *Cotton Supreme Sapling*
  (#5 bulky weight; 100% organic cotton;
  each approximately 3½ oz/100 g and 109
  yd/100 m): 3 (3, 4, 4) hanks of Aqua #516
- Knitting needles, US size 9 (5.5 mm) or size
  needed to obtain gauge
- 2 US 9 (5.5 mm) double-pointed knitting
  needles or size needed to obtain gauge
- 6 Buttons, ⅞ in/2.25 cm diameter

GAUGE

In Garter Rib Pattern, 13 stitches and 24 rows
= 4 in/10 cm, blocked.

To save time, take time to check gauge.

Garter Rib (Multiple of 2 Stitches + 1 Stitch)
Row 1 (RS): *K1, p1; repeat from the * across,
ending with k1.

Row 2: Purl across.

Repeat Rows 1 and 2 for the pattern.

HOODIE

BACK
Cast on 37 (41, 45, 47) stitches.

Begin the Garter Rib Pattern and work even until the piece measures approximately 6 (6½, 7¼, 8) in/15 (16.5, 18.5, 20.5) cm from the beginning, ending after WS row.

Shape Armholes
Bind off 2 (2, 3, 3) stitches at the beginning of the next 2 rows, then use the k2tog technique to decrease 1 stitch each side every row 2 (3, 3, 2) times, then every other row 2 (2, 2, 3) times—25 (27, 29, 31) stitches remain.

Continue even in the pattern as established until the piece measures approximately 10½ (11½, 12½, 13½) in/26.5 (29, 32, 34.5) cm from the beginning, ending after WS row.

Shape Shoulders
Bind off 3 (4, 4, 5) stitches at the beginning of the next 2 rows, then bind off 3 (3, 4, 4) stitches at the beginning of the next 2 rows— 13 stitches remain.

Bind off in the pattern.

LEFT FRONT
Cast on 25 (27, 29, 31) stitches.

Begin the Garter Rib Pattern and work even until the piece measures approximately 6 (6½, 7¼, 8) in/15 (16.5, 18.5, 20.5) cm from the beginning, ending after WS row.

Shape Armhole
Bind off 2 (2, 3, 3) stitches at the beginning of the next row, then use the k2tog technique to decrease 1 stitch at the armhole edge every

row 2 (3, 3, 2) times, then every other row 2 (2, 2, 3) times—19 (20, 21, 23) stitches remain.

Continue even in the pattern as established until the piece measures approximately 8¼ (9¼, 10¼, 11¼) in/21 (23.5, 26, 28.5) cm from the beginning, ending after a RS row.

Shape Neck
Bind off 8 (8, 8, 9) stitches at the beginning of the next row, then bind off 2 stitches at the neck edge twice, then use the k2tog technique to decrease 1 stitch at neck edge once—6 (7, 8, 9) stitches remain.

Continue even until the piece measures the same as the back to the shoulders, ending after a WS row.

Shape Shoulders
Bind off 3 (4, 4, 5) stitches at the shoulder edge once.

Work 1 row even.

Bind off 3 (3, 4, 4) stitches.

Place markers for 6 buttons as shown in photograph.

RIGHT FRONT
Same as left front, reversing armhole shaping, until the piece measures approximately 8¼ (9¼, 10¼, 11¼) in/21 (23.5, 26, 28.5) cm from the beginning, ending after a WS row, **and at the same time,** make 6 buttonholes on RS rows opposite markers as follows: Work 2 stitches in the pattern as established, bind off 2 stitches, work pattern as established across to end the row. On the next row, cast on 2 stitches over each set of bound-off stitches.

Shape Neck
Bind off 8 (8, 8, 9) stitches at the beginning of the next row, then bind off 3 stitches at the neck edge once, bind off 2 stitches at the neck edge once, then use the k2tog technique to decrease 1 stitch at the neck edge every row twice—6 (7, 8, 9) stitches remain.

Continue even until the piece measures the same as the back to the shoulders, ending after a RS row.

Shape Shoulders
Same as for Left Front.

SLEEVES (MAKE 2)
Cast on 25 (25, 27, 27) stitches.

Begin the Garter Rib Pattern, and use the K1f&b technique (page 141) to increase 1 stitch each side every 8 rows 0 (1, 0, 0) times, then every 10 rows 2 (2, 3, 3) times—29 (31, 33, 33) stitches.

Continue even until the piece measures approximately 4¾ (5¾, 6¾, 7¾) in/12 (14.5, 17, 19.5) cm from the beginning, ending after WS row.

Shape Cap
Bind off 2 (2, 3, 3) stitches at the beginning of the next 2 rows, then use the k2tog technique to decrease 1 stitch each side every 4 rows 0 (0, 0, 1) time, every other row 5 (6, 7, 6) times, then every row 1 (1, 0, 0) time—13 stitches remain.

Bind off 2 stitches at the beginning of the next 4 rows—5 stitches remain.

Bind off.

Finishing
Darn in all yarn tails.

Block pieces to measurements.

HOOD
With RS facing, begin and end 2½ in/6.5 cm in from front neck edge, pick up and knit 29 stitches along the neckline.

Row 1 (WS): Purl across. Place a marker on the middle stitch.

Row 2 (Increase Row): Work Garter Stitch across to 1 stitch before the marked stitch, Kf&b (page 141), k1 (the marked stitch), Kf&b, work the pattern as established across to end the row—31 stitches.

Work 3 rows even in the pattern, keeping the center stitch as knit on the RS and purl on the WS, incorporating the increased stitches into the pattern as established.

Repeat the last 4 rows 4 more times—39 stitches.

Continue even in the pattern as established until the hood measures approximately 4½ in/11.5 cm from the beginning, ending after a WS row.

Next Row (RS) (Decrease Row): Work the pattern as established until 2 stitches before the marked stitch, ssk, k1 (the marked stitch), k2tog, work the pattern as established across to end the row—37 stitches remain.

Work 3 rows even in the pattern, keeping the center stitch as knit on the RS and purl on the WS.

Repeat the last 4 rows 4 *more* times—29 stitches remain.

Next Row (WS): Work even in the pattern as established.

Next Row: Work the Decrease Row—27 stitches remain.

Repeat the last 2 rows once more—25 stitches remain.

Next Row (WS): Work the pattern as established across the first 17 stitches, p2tog, work the pattern as established across to end the row—24 stitches remain.

Divide the remaining stitches onto two double-pointed needles, putting 12 stitches onto each one and holding RS facing each other, seam together using the three-needle bind-off technique (page 155).

Sew in sleeves.

Sew side and sleeve seams.

Garter Rib

(WS) 2 | | | 1 (RS)

☐ = Knit on RS; purl on WS

• = Purl on RS; knit on WS

☐ = Stitch and row repeat

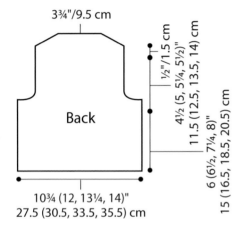

3¾"/9.5 cm

Back

½"/1.5 cm

4½ (5, 5¼, 5½)"
11.5 (12.5, 13.5, 14) cm

6 (6½, 7¼, 8)"
15 (16.5, 18.5, 20.5) cm

10¾ (12, 13¼, 14)"
27.5 (30.5, 33.5, 35.5) cm

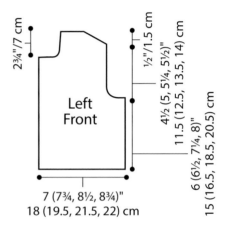

Left Front

2¾"/7 cm

½"/1.5 cm

4½ (5, 5¼, 5½)"
11.5 (12.5, 13.5, 14) cm

6 (6½, 7¼, 8)"
15 (16.5, 18.5, 20.5) cm

7 (7¾, 8½, 8¾)"
18 (19.5, 21.5, 22) cm

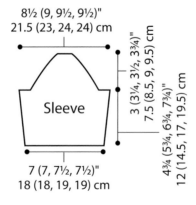

8½ (9, 9½, 9½)"
21.5 (23, 24, 24) cm

Sleeve

3 (3¼, 3½, 3¾)"
7.5 (8.5, 9, 9.5) cm

4¾ (5¾, 6¾, 7¾)"
12 (14.5, 17, 19.5) cm

7 (7, 7½, 7½)"
18 (18, 19, 19) cm

Rocking Horse Bib

#InstaKnitsForBaby_RockingHorseBib

TIME TO KNIT 6 hours

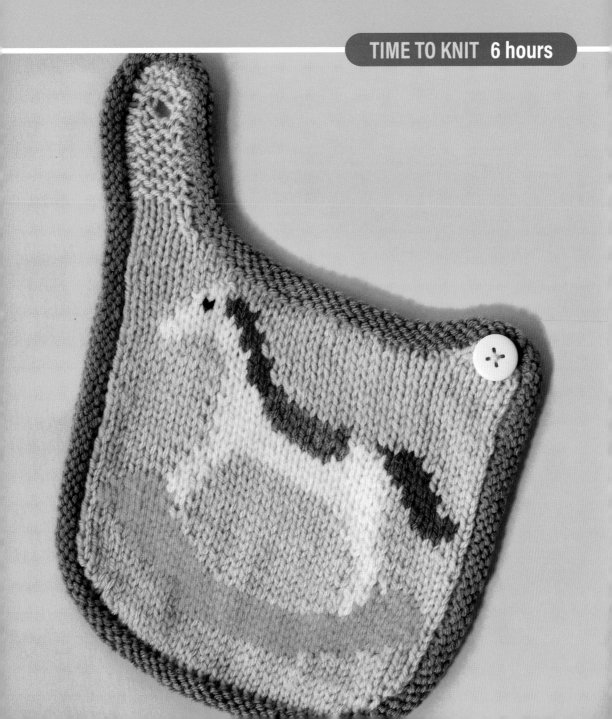

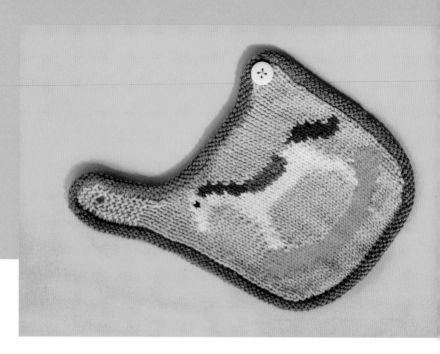

SIZES
One size

FINISHED MEASUREMENTS
Height: 8½ in/21.5 cm plus straps
Width: 8¼ in/21 cm

MATERIALS
- Lion Brand *Vanna's Choice* (#4 medium weight; 100% acrylic; each approximately 3½ oz/100 g and 170 yd/156 m), 1 ball each of #1787 Seaglass (A), #104 Grapefruit (B), #098 Fisherman (C), #125 Taupe (D), and #177 Sage (E)
- Knitting needles, US size 9 (5.5 mm) or size needed to obtain gauge
- Circular knitting needle, US size 8 (5 mm), 16 in/40 cm in length
- 2 Stitch markers
- 1 Button

GAUGE
In Stockinette Stitch, 16 stitches and 22 rows = 4 in/10 cm, blocked.

To save time, take time to check gauge.

NOTES:
- *This project is knitted using intarsia technique (page 139).*
- *For fully fashioned increases on right-side rows, k1, M1 (page 144), work the patterns across as established to the last stitch, ending with M1, k1.*
- *For fully fashioned decreases on right-side rows, k1, ssk (page 153), work the patterns across as established to the last 3 stitches, ending with k2tog, k1.*

Stockinette Stitch (Over Any Number of Stitches)

Row 1 (RS): Knit across.

Row 2: Purl across.

Repeat Rows 1 and 2 for the pattern.

Rocking Horse Pattern (Over 29 Stitches)
See the chart.

Rocking Horse Pattern

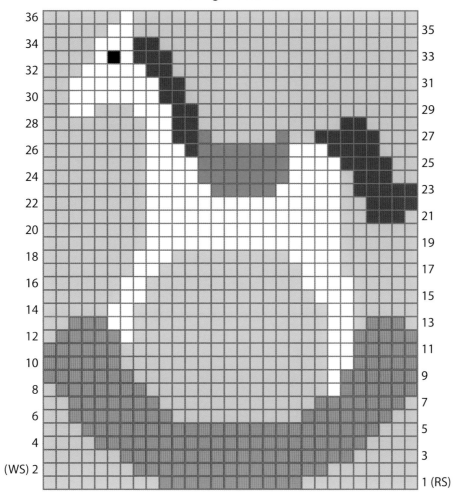

36 · 35 · 34 · 33 · 32 · 31 · 30 · 29 · 28 · 27 · 26 · 25 · 24 · 23 · 22 · 21 · 20 · 19 · 18 · 17 · 16 · 15 · 14 · 13 · 12 · 11 · 10 · 9 · 8 · 7 · 6 · 5 · 4 · 3 · (WS) 2 · 1 (RS)

Color Key

☐ = A

▨ = B

☐ = C

■ = D

▩ = E

BIB

With A, cast on 21 stitches.

Begin Stockinette Stitch and cast on 2 stitches at the beginning of each of the next 4 rows, then work fully fashioned increases (see Notes) each side on the next row and then on the next right-side row and on the next row begin working the Rocking Horse Pattern over the middle 29 stitches, with markers on each side—33 stitches.

Continue even in the patterns as established until Row 36 of the Rocking Horse Pattern is completed.

Shape Neck

Work across the first 12 stitches, join a second ball of A and bind off the middle 9 stitches, work across to end the row.

Continue with separate balls of A and bind off 3 stitches each neck edge once, bind off 2 stitches each neck edge once, then work fully fashioned decreases (see Notes) each side once—6 stitches remain each side.

Next Row (RS): Bind off 6 stitches; with the second ball of yarn, k6 on the other side of neck.

Continue in Garter Stitch on these 6 stitches until the strap measures approximately 11¼ in/28.5 cm from the beginning.

Next Row (Buttonhole Row): K2, bind off the next 2 stitches, k2.

Continue in Garter Stitch, using the e-wrap technique (page 134) to cast on 2 stitches above the bound-off stitches on the previous row, for ¾ in/2 cm more.

Bind off.

Finishing

With the RS facing, A, and the circular needle, begin at shorter shoulder edge and pick up and knit stitches around the neck edge to the edge of the other shoulder edge as follows: 1 stitch for every stitch along horizontal sections and 3 stitches for every 4 rows along vertical sections.

Change to E and purl 2 rows.

Next Row: Knit 1 row.

Next Row: Purl 1 row.

Knit as you bind off.

Block piece to the final measurements.

Sew button ¾ in/2 cm down on the shorter shoulder.

Honey Bunny

#InstaKnitsForBaby_HoneyBunny

TIME TO KNIT 6½ hours

FINISHED MEASUREMENTS
Height: 10 in/25.5 cm,
excluding ears

MATERIALS
- Manos del Uruguay *Alegria Grande* (#4 medium weight; 75% superwash merino wool/ 25% polyamide; 3½ oz/100 g and 219 yd/200 m), 1 hank each of Natural #AG2800 (A) and Petal #AG2149 (B)
- 1 yd/m of black yarn or embroidery floss
- Knitting needles, US size 8 (5 mm) or size needed to obtain gauge
- Stitch holders
- Fiberfill stuffing

GAUGE
In Stockinette Stitch, 18 stitches and 24 rows = 4 in/10 cm.

To save time, take time to check gauge.

BUNNY

FIRST LEG
With A, cast on 12 stitches.

Row 1 (RS): Kf&b (page 141) across— 24 stitches.

Row 2: Purl across.

Row 3: Knit across.

Row 4 and 5: As Rows 2 and 3.

Row 6: As Row 2.

Row 7: K12, M1 (page 144), k12, turn— 25 stitches.

Row 8: Slip the first stitch purlwise with the yarn in front, p4, p2tog, turn—24 stitches.

Row 9: Slip the first stitch purlwise with the yarn in back, k4, ssk, turn—23 stitches.

Rows 10–19: As Rows 8 and 9—13 stitches remain after Row 19.

Row 20: Slip the first stitch purlwise with the yarn in front, p4, p2tog, p2—12 stitches.

Row 21: Knit across.

Row 22: Purl across.

Rows 23–30: As Rows 21 and 22.

Row 31: As Row 21. Cut the yarn, leaving an 8 in/20.5 cm tail.

Slip these 12 stitches onto a holder.

SECOND LEG
Same as first leg. Once Row 31 is completed, do not cut the yarn.

BODY AND HEAD
Row 32 (WS): P12 from the second leg and with the WS facing, p12 from the first leg—24 stitches.

Row 33: K2, M1 (page 144), k9, M1, k2, M1, k9, M1, k2—28 stitches.

Row 34: Purl across.

Row 35: K2, M1, k10, M1, k4, M1, K10, M1, k2—32 stitches.

Row 36: Purl across.

Row 37: K2, M1, k11, M1, k6, M1, k11, M1, k2—36 stitches.

Row 38: Purl across.

Row 39: Knit across.

Rows 40–43: As Rows 38 and 39.

Row 44: As Row 38.

Row 45: K12, k2tog, k8, ssk, k12—34 stitches.

Row 46: Purl across.

Row 47: K8, bind off the next 4 stitches, knit across until 12 stitches remain in the row, bind off the next 4 stitches, knit across to end the row.

Row 48: Purl across and cast on 4 stitches over the bound-off stitches of the previous row.

Row 49: K2, ssk, k7, k2tog, k8, ssk, k7, k2tog, k2—30 stitches.

Row 50: Purl across.

Row 51: Knit across.

Row 52: [P2tog] 15 times—15 stitches remain.

Row 53: [K1, M1] 14 times, k1—29 stitches.

Row 54: Purl across.

Row 55: [K2, M1] 14 times, k1—43 stitches.

Row 56: Purl across.

Row 57: K4, [M1, k7] 5 times, M1, k4—49 stitches.

Row 58: Purl across.

Row 59: Knit across.

Row 60: As Row 58.

Row 61: K21, sssk (page 154), k1, k3tog, k21—45 stitches.

Row 62: Purl across.

Row 63: K19, sssk, k1, k3tog, k19—41 stitches.

Row 64: Purl across.

Row 65: K2, ssk, k13, sssk, k1, k3tog, k13, k2tog, k2—35 stitches.

Row 66: Purl across.

Row 67: K2, ssk, k10, sssk, k1, k3tog, k10, k2tog, k2—29 stitches.

Row 68: Purl across.

Row 69: K2, ssk, k7, sssk, k1, k3tog, k7, k2tog, k2—23 stitches.

Row 70: Purl across.

Row 71: K2, ssk, k1, [ssk] 3 times, k1, [k2tog] 3 times, k1, k2tog, k2—15 stitches.

Row 72: Purl across.

Row 73: [K2tog] 7 times, k1—8 stitches.

Cut the yarn, leaving a 24 in/61 cm tail for sewing.

Thread the tail through the remaining 8 stitches and pull tight.

ARM (MAKE 2)
Row 1 (RS): With the RS facing, begin at the third of the 4 bound-off stitches of one armhole and pick up and knit 2 stitches on the bind-off edge, pick up and knit 1 stitch in the corner, pick up and knit 4 stitches along the top cast-on edge of the armhole, pick up and knit 1 stitch in the corner, pick up and knit 2 stitches on the bind-off edge—10 stitches.

Row 2: Purl across.

Row 3: Knit across.

Rows 4–19: As Rows 2 and 3.

Row 20: As Row 2.

Row 21: [K2tog] 5 times—5 stitches.

Cut the yarn, leaving an 8 in/20.5 cm tail.

Thread the tail through the 10 stitches and pull tightly.

Sew the seams, stuffing as you go.

EAR (MAKE 2 EACH IN BOTH A AND B)
Cast on 5 stitches.

Row 1 (RS): Knit across.

Row 2 and all WS rows except Row 34: Purl across.

Row 3: K2, M1, k1, M1, k2—7 stitches.

Row 5: K3, M1, k1, M1, k3—9 stitches.

Row 7: K4, M1, k1, M1, k4—11 stitches.

Row 9: K5, M1, k1, M1, k5—13 stitches.

Rows 11, 13, 15, 17, 19, 21, and 25: Knit across.

Rows 23, 27, 29, and 31: K1, ssk, knit across to the last 3 stitches, ending with k2tog, k1—5 stitches remain after Row 31.

Row 33: K1, s2kp2 (page 152), k1—3 stitches.

Row 34: P3tog.

Cut the yarn, leaving a 12 in/30.5 cm tail.

With the WS of one ear made with A facing the WS of an ear made with B, use mattress stitch to sew the 2 layers together.

Repeat for the other 2 ears.

Sew ears onto the head as seen in the photo.

Make pom-pom for tail. Attach to bunny.

Naptime Blankie

#InstaKnitsForBaby_NaptimeBlankie

TIME TO KNIT **10 hours**

FINISHED MEASUREMENTS

36 × 36 in/91.5 × 91.5 cm

MATERIALS

- Lion Brand *Wool Ease Thick and Quick* (#6 super bulky weight; 80% acrylic/20% wool; each approximately 5 oz/140 g and 87 yd/80 m), 8 balls of Carousel #619
- Circular knitting needle, US size 13 (9 mm) or size needed to obtain gauge, 40 in/101 cm in length
- Stitch marker

GAUGE

In Stockinette Stitch, 10 stitches and 13 rows = 4 in/10 cm, blocked.

To save time, take time to check gauge.

BLANKET

Cast on 169 stitches. Place a split ring marker on the middle stitch.

Row 1 (WS): Slip the first stitch knitwise (page 144), knit across to the center marked stitch, p1, knit across to the last stitch, ending with p1.

Row 2: Slip the first stitch knitwise, knit across to 1 stitch before the center marked stitch, s2kp2 (page 152), knit across to the last stitch, ending with p1—2 stitches decreased.

Row 3: Slip the first stitch knitwise, purl across to end the row.

Row 4: As Row 2.

Row 5: As Row 1.

Repeat Rows 2–5 until 3 stitches remain.

Next Row: S2kp2.

Fasten off.

Finishing

Darn in all yarn tails.

Block the piece to finished measurements.

Koala Lovey

#InstaKnitsForBaby_KoalaLovey

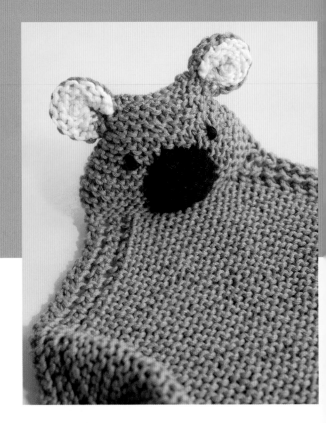

SIZES
One size

FINISHED MEASUREMENTS
Height: 24¼ in/64 cm
Width: 23 in/58.5 cm

MATERIALS
- Berroco *Comfort Chunky* (#5 bulky weight; 50% nylon/50% acrylic; each approximately 3½ oz/100 g and 150 yd/137 m), 2 skeins of Ash Gray #5770 (A) and 1 skein each of Ivory #5701 (B) and Liquorice #5734 (C)
- Circular knitting needle, US size 10½ (6.5 mm) or size needed to obtain gauge
- Double-pointed knitting needles, US size 10½ (6.5 mm) or size needed to obtain gauge
- Fiberfill stuffing

GAUGE
In Garter Stitch, 15 stitches and 30 rows = 4 in/10 cm, blocked.

To save time, take time to check gauge.

NOTES:
- *This blanket is worked on the diagonal.*
- *The circular knitting needle is used to accommodate the large number of stitches. Do not join at the end of rows; instead, work back and forth in rows.*

Garter Stitch (Over Any Number of Stitches)
Row 1 (RS): Knit across.

Row 2: Knit across.

Repeat Rows 1 and 2 for the pattern.

LOVEY

BLANKET

With A, work same as the Teddy Bear Lovey Blanket (pages 54–57).

HEAD

Continue with A, work same as the Teddy Bear Lovey Head (pages 56–57).

EARS (MAKE 2)

With A, cast on 5 stitches.

Row 1 (RS): Kf&b (page 141), k3, kf&b— 7 stitches.

Row 2: Kf&b, k5, kf&b—9 stitches.

Row 3: Knit across.

Row 4: Kf&b, k7, kf&b—11 stitches.

Row 5: Knit across.

Row 6: Kf&b, k9, kf&b—13 stitches.

Rows 7 and 8: Knit across.

Rows 9 and 10: Change to B, knit across.

Row 11: Continuing with B for the rest of the ear, k3tog, k7, k3tog—9 stitches.

Row 12: Knit across.

Row 13: K2tog, k5, k2tog—7 stitches.

Knit as you bind off.

Fold each ear in half and seam the side edges. Seam the beginning and end of the wide edge together to form the base of the ears.

SNOUT (MAKE 1)

With C, cast on 2 stitches.

Row 1: [Kf&b] twice—4 stitches.

Row 2: K1, [kf&b] twice, k1—6 stitches.

Row 3: K1, kf&b, k2, kf&b, k1—8 stitches.

Rows 4–10: Knit across.

Row 11: K1, k2tog, k2, k2tog, k1—6 stitches.

Row 12: K1, [k2tog] twice, k1—4 stitches.

Row 13: [K2tog] twice—2 stitches.

Knit as you bind off.

Finishing

Sew the snout onto the RS of the head, stuffing as you go.

Use the black yarn or embroidery floss to embroider the eyes as shown in the photograph.

Sew on the ears as shown in the photograph.

Stuff the head. Sew the back side and lower head seam.

Darn in all remaining yarn tails.

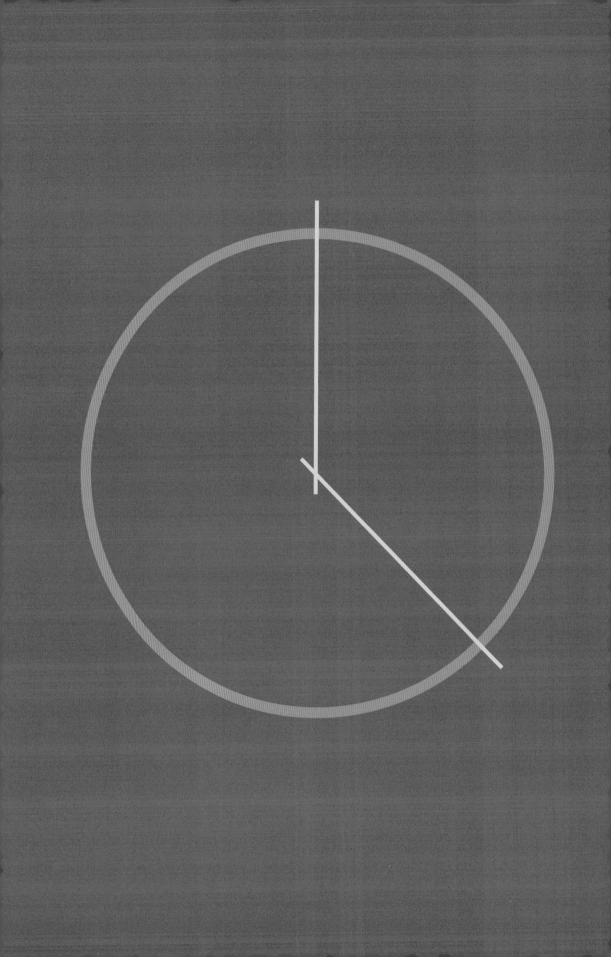

TEN TO TWENTY HOURS

Do you have a trip scheduled to visit the in-laws? You can whip up most of the designs in this section while cruising on I-95 while Hubby drives.

#RoadTrip #TravelingKnitters

#KnittingOnTheRoad

Confetti Jacket

#InstaKnitsForBaby_ConfettiJacket

TIME TO KNIT 11 to 13 hours, depending on the size

SIZES

6 Months (12 Months, 18 Months, 24 Months). Instructions are for the smallest size, with changes for other sizes noted in parentheses as necessary.

FINISHED MEASUREMENTS

Chest: 20 (21, 22, 23) in/51 (53.5, 56, 58.5) cm, closed

Length: 10 (10½, 11, 11½) in/25.5 (26.5, 28, 29) cm

MATERIALS

- Koigu *Chelsea* (#4 medium weight; 100% superwash merino wool; each approximately 3½ oz/100 g and 125 yd/114 m): 3 (3, 4) hanks of #534
- Knitting needles, US size 8 (5 mm) or size needed to obtain gauge
- 2 US 8 (5 mm) double-pointed knitting needles or size needed to obtain gauge
- 1 Snap, ¾ in/20 mm in diameter
- Stitch markers

GAUGE

In Stockinette Stitch, 16 stitches and 24 rows = 4 in/10 cm, blocked.

To save time, take time to check gauge.

NOTES:

- *For a fully fashioned decrease at the beginning of a row, on right-side rows, k1, ssk (page 153), continue across to end the row; on wrong-side rows, p1, p2tog (page 145), continue across to end the row.*
- *For a fully fashioned decrease at the end of a row, on right-side rows, work across until 3 stitches remain in the row, ending the row with k2tog (page 143), k1; on wrong-side rows, work across until 3 stitches remain in the row, ending the row with ssp (page 154), p1.*
- *For fully fashioned increases, k1, M1 (page 144), work across until 1 stitch remains in the row, ending the row with M1, k1.*

Stockinette Stitch

Row 1 (RS): Knit across.

Row 2: Purl across.

Repeat Rows 1 and 2 for the pattern.

JACKET

BACK
Cast on 42 (44, 46, 48) stitches.

Begin Stockinette Stitch and work even until the piece measures approximately 10 (10½, 11, 11½) in/25.5 (26.5, 28, 29) cm from the beginning, ending after WS row.

Bind off.

RIGHT FRONT
Cast on 36 (38, 42, 42) stitches.

Begin Stockinette Stitch and work even until the piece measures approximately 3 (3½, 3½, 4) in/7.5 (9, 9, 10) cm from the beginning, ending after WS row.

Work fully fashioned decreases at the neck on the next row and every row 9 (11, 15, 13) times, then every other row 13 (12, 11, 12) times—13 (14, 15, 16) stitches remain.

Work even until the piece measures approximately 10 (10½, 11, 11½) in/25.5 (26.5, 28, 29) cm from the beginning, ending After WS row.

Bind off.

LEFT FRONT
Same as Right Front, reversing all shaping.

SLEEVE (MAKE 2)
Cast on 29 (29, 32, 32) stitches.

Begin Stockinette Stitch and work fully fashioned increases (see Notes) each side every 4 rows 1 (3, 2, 1) time(s), then every 6 rows 3 (2, 3, 4) times—37 (39, 42, 42) stitches.

Continue even until the piece measures approximately 4¾ (5, 5¼, 5¾) in/12 (12.5, 13.5, 14.5) cm from the beginning, ending after WS row.

Bind off.

Finishing
Block pieces to finished measurements.

Darn in yarn tails.

Sew the shoulder seams.

Place markers 4½ (4¾, 5, 5) in/11.5 (12, 12.5, 12.5) cm down from the shoulders on Fronts and Back.

Set in the sleeves between the markers.

SLEEVE EDGING
With the RS facing, pick up and knit 29 (29, 32, 32) stitches along the lower edge of the sleeve.

Next Row (WS): Knit across.

Next Row: Purl across.

Next Row: Knit as you bind off.

Repeat for the second sleeve.

Sew the side and sleeve seams.

FRONT AND NECKLINE EDGING
With the RS facing, begin at the lower Right Front edge and pick up and knit 12 (14, 14,

16) stitches along the flat section of the Right Front, place a marker, pick up and knit 28 (28, 30, 30) stitches along the Right Front neck opening, pick up and knit 18 stitches along the back of the neck, pick up and knit 28 (28, 30, 30) stitches along the Left Front neck opening, place a marker, pick up and knit 12 (14, 14, 16) stitches along the flat section of Left Front—98 (102, 106, 110) stitches.

Next Row (WS): Knit across to the marker, slip the marker, M1 knitwise, knit to the next marker, M1 knitwise, slip the marker, knit across to end the row.

Next Row: Purl across.

Next Row: Bind off as you knit across to the first marker, M1 knitwise, bind off as you knit across to the next marker, M1 knitwise, bind off as you knit across to end the row.

LOWER BODY EDGING
With RS facing, and circular needle, pick up and knit 110 (116, 126, 128) stitches along the lower edge of Left Front, Back, and Right Front.

Complete the same as the sleeve edging.

Sew the snap to the inside of Right Front and outside of Left Front as seen in the photo.

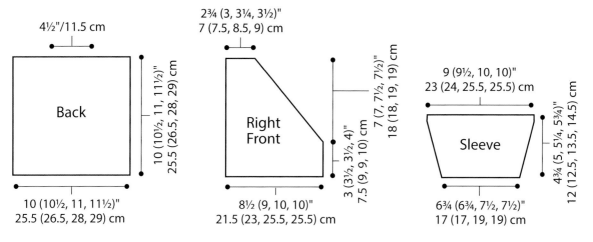

4½"/11.5 cm

Back

10 (10½, 11, 11½)"
25.5 (26.5, 28, 29) cm

10 (10½, 11, 11½)"
25.5 (26.5, 28, 29) cm

2¾ (3, 3¼, 3½)"
7 (7.5, 8.5, 9) cm

Right Front

7 (7, 7½, 7½)"
18 (18, 19, 19) cm

3 (3½, 3½, 4)"
7.5 (9, 9, 10) cm

8½ (9, 10, 10)"
21.5 (23, 25.5, 25.5) cm

9 (9½, 10, 10)"
23 (24, 25.5, 25.5) cm

Sleeve

4¾ (5, 5¼, 5¾)"
12 (12.5, 13.5, 14.5) cm

6¾ (6¾, 7½, 7½)"
17 (17, 19, 19) cm

Snug as a Bug in a Rug Bunting

#InstaKnitsforBaby_
SnugAsABugInARugBunting

TIME TO KNIT 11 hours

SIZES
One size to fit Newborn/3 Months

FINISHED MEASUREMENTS
17 × 22 in/43 × 56 cm, excluding hood

MATERIALS
- Cascade Yarn *Pacific Chunky* (#5 bulky weight; 60% acrylic/40% superwash merino wool; each approximately 3½ oz/100 g and 120 yd/110 m), 4 balls of Cranberry #119
- Knitting needles, US size 10½ (6.5 mm) or size needed to obtain gauge
- Stitch markers
- 10 Buttons, 1 in/25 mm diameter

GAUGE
In Stockinette Stitch, 13 stitches and 20 rows = 4 in/10 cm, blocked.

To save time, take time to check gauge.

Stockinette Stitch
Row 1 (RS): Knit across.

Row 2: Purl across.

Repeat Rows 1 and 2 for the pattern.

Double Seed Stitch (Over an Odd Number of Stitches)
Row 1 (RS): *K1, p1; repeat from the * across, ending with k1.

Row 2: *P1, k1; repeat from the * across, ending with p1.

Row 3: As Row 2.

Row 4: As Row 1.

Repeat Rows 1–4 for the pattern.

NOTE:
- *For buttonholes work 3 stitches in the pattern as established, bind off the next 2 stitches, continue across the row in the patterns as established until 5 stitches remain. End with binding off the next 2 stitches and working 3 stitches in the pattern as established. On the next row, use the e-wrap method (page 134) to cast on 2 stitches over the bound-off stitches.*

BUNTING

Cast on 55 stitches.

Setup Row (RS): Work Row 1 of Double Seed Stitch across the first 7 stitches, place a marker, knit across to the last 7 stitches, place a marker, ending with Row 1 of Double Seed Stitch to end the row.

Continue even in the patterns as established, slipping markers as you come to them, until the piece measures approximately 8 in/20.5 cm from the beginning, ending after WS row.

Place a marker on each side edge for end of hood section.

Continue even in the patterns as established until the piece measures approximately 31 in/78.5 cm from the beginning.

Make buttonholes each side (see Note) on the next row.

Continue even in the patterns as established until the piece measures approximately 36 in/91.5 cm from the beginning.

Make buttonholes each side on the next row.

Continue even in the patterns as established until the piece measures approximately 41 in/104 cm from the beginning.

Make buttonholes each side on the next row.

Continue even in the patterns as established until the piece measures approximately 46 in/117 cm from the beginning.

Make buttonholes each side on the next row.

Continue even in the patterns as established until the piece measures approximately 50 in/127 cm from the beginning.

Begin working Double Seed Stitch as established across all stitches and work even until the piece measures approximately 51 in/129.5 cm from the beginning.

Make buttonholes each side on the next row.

Continue even in the patterns as established until the piece measures approximately 52 in/132 cm from the beginning.

Bind off in the pattern.

Finishing

Block to the finished measurements.

Fold 8 in/20.5 cm at each side together to form hood (see Assembly Diagram).

Sew hood seam.

Fold bind-off row up to meet the top set of markers (see Assembly Diagram).

Sew buttons to match the buttonholes.

Assembly Diagram

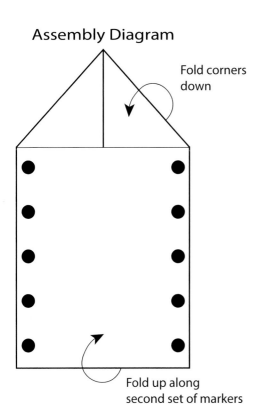

Fold corners down

Fold up along second set of markers

Direction of Knitting

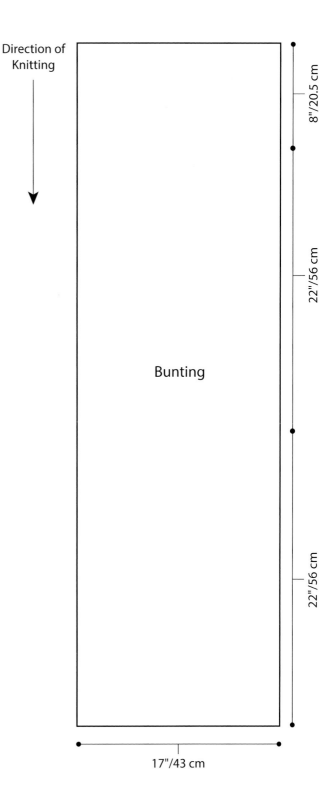

Bunting

8"/20.5 cm

22"/56 cm

22"/56 cm

17"/43 cm

Sunny Topper

#InstaKnitsForBaby_SunnyTopper

TIME TO KNIT 16 to 18 hours, depending on the size

SIZES

3–6 Months (6–9 Months, 9–12 Months). Instructions are for the smallest size, with changes for other sizes noted in parentheses as necessary.

FINISHED MEASUREMENTS

Chest: 23 (25½, 27) in/58.5 (65, 68.5) cm
Length: 7½ (9½, 11¼) in/19 (24, 28.5) cm

MATERIALS

- Berroco *Ultra Wool Chunky* (#5 bulky weight; 100% superwash wool; each approximately 3½ oz/100 g and 145 yd/133 m), 2 (2, 3) balls of Butter #4312
- Circular knitting needle, US size 9 (5.5 mm) or size needed to obtain gauge, 16 in/40 cm in length
- Double-pointed knitting needles, US size 9 (5.5 mm) or size needed to obtain gauge
- 8 stitch markers
- 2 stitch holders
- 3 buttons, ¾ in/20 mm diameter

GAUGE

In Stockinette Stitch, 16 stitches and 24 rows = 4 in/10 cm, blocked.

To save time, take time to check gauge.

NOTES:

- *This design is made from the neck down; the front and bottom borders are knitted at the same time as the body.*
- *The circular needle is used to accommodate the larger number of stitches; do not join; work back and forth in rows.*
- *Make the second and third buttonholes 10 (12, 14) rows after the previous buttonhole.*

TOPPER

BODY
Cast on 48 (52, 56) stitches.

Row 1 (RS): Knit across.

Rows 2, 5, 10, 16, and 17: Knit across.

Row 3 (First Buttonhole Row): K4. place a marker, knit across to the last 4 stitches, k2tog, yarn over, k2, place a marker; knit last 4 stitches.

Row 4: Slipping markers as you come to them, knit across, and use the M1 technique (page 144) to increase 39 (43, 47) stitches evenly spaced between the markers—87 (95, 103) stitches.

Rows 6, 7, 8, 12, 13, 14, and 18: K4, slip marker, purl across to the next marker, slip marker, k4.

Rows 9 and 15: K4, slip marker, k1, *yarn over, k2tog; repeat from the * across to the next marker, slip marker, k4.

Row 11: Slipping markers as you come to them, knit across, and use the M1 technique to increase 34 stitches evenly spaced between the markers—121 (129, 137) stitches.

For Size 3–6 Months Only
Rows 19 and 21: Knit across.

Row 20: K4, purl across to the last 4 stitches, ending with k4.

Row 22 (WS): Slipping markers as you come to them, k12, [kf&b (page 141), k7] 15 times, k4—136 stitches.

For Size 6–9 Months Only
Rows 19, 20, 22, 23, 25, 26, 29, 30, and 31: Knit across.

Rows 21 and 27: As Row 9.

Row 24: As Row 6.

Row 28: Slipping markers as you come to them, k13, [kf&b, k3] 26 times, kf&b, k11—156 stitches.

For Size 9–12 Months Only
Rows 19–27: Same as for Size 6–9 Months.

Rows 28–31: Slipping markers as you come to them, knit across.

Row 32: K9, [kf&b, k3] 31 times, k4—168 stitches.

For All Sizes
Divide for Lower Body and Sleeves

Next Row (RS): Removing markers as you come to them, k20 (23, 25) for the Left Front, slip the next 30 (35, 38) stitches onto a holder for Sleeve, cast on 4 stitches for the Underarm, k36 (40, 42) stitches for Back, slip the next 30 (35, 38) stitches onto a holder for Sleeve, cast on 4 stitches for underarm, k20 (23, 25) stitches for the Right Front.

Next Row (WS): K4, purl across until 4 stitches remain, ending the row with k4.

Next Row (RS): Knit across.

Repeat the last 2 rows until the piece measures approximately 3 (4, 5) in/7.5 (10, 12.5) cm from the underarm, or until ¾ in/2 cm less than the desired total finished length, ending after WS row.

Next 4 Rows: Knit all stitches.

Bind off knitwise.

SLEEVES
Using the double-pointed needles, pick up 4 stitches along the underarm, then k30 (35, 38) stitches from the stitch holder—34 (39, 42) stitches.

Next 6 Rounds: Alternate 1 knit round with 1 purl round for garter stitch.

Bind off.

Finishing
Darn in all yarn tails.

Block piece to measurements.

Sew on buttons opposite buttonholes.

All Dressed Up

#InstaKnitsForBaby_AllDressedUp

TIME TO KNIT 11 to 13 hours, depending on the size

SIZES
0–3 Months (3–6 Months, 6–9 Months, 12 Months, 24 Months). Instructions are for the smallest size, with changes for other sizes noted in parentheses as necessary.

FINISHED MEASUREMENTS
Chest: 20 (21, 22, 23½, 24½) in/51 (53.5, 56, 59.5, 62) cm
Length: 15 (15½, 16, 16½, 17½) in/38 (39.5, 40.5, 42, 44.5) cm

MATERIALS
- Koigu *KPM* (#1 fingering weight; 100% superwash merino wool; each approximately 1¾ oz/50 g and 175 yd/160 m): 3 (3, 3, 4, 4) hanks of #1162
- Knitting needles, US size 3 (3.25 mm) or size needed to obtain gauge

GAUGE
In Stockinette Stitch, 28 stitches and 36 rows = 4 in/10 cm, blocked.

To save time, take time to check gauge.

K2P2 Rib (Over Multiple of 4 + 2 Stitches)
Row 1 (RS): *K2, p2; repeat from the * across, ending with k2.

Row 2: *P2, k2; repeat from the * across, ending with p2.

Repeat Rows 1 and 2 for the pattern.

Stockinette Stitch
Row 1 (RS): Knit across.

Row 2: Purl across.

Repeat Rows 1 and 2 for the pattern.

NOTES:
- *For single fully fashioned decreases, on RS rows, k1, ssk (page 153), work across to the last 3 stitches, ending with k2tog, k1; on WS rows, p1, p2tog, work across to the last 3 stitches, ending with ssp (page 154), p1.*
- *For double fully fashioned decreases, on RS rows, k1, sssk (page 154), work across to the last 4 stitches, ending with k3tog, k1.*

DRESS

BACK
Cast on 106 (110, 114, 118, 122) stitches.

Begin K2P2 Rib and work even until the piece measures approximately ¾ in/2 cm from the beginning.

Begin Stockinette Stitch and work single fully fashioned decreases (see Notes) every 4 rows 11 (10, 8, 7, 4) times, then every 6 rows 7 (8, 10, 11, 14) times—70 (74, 78, 82, 86) stitches remain.

Knit 2 rows.

Begin K2P2 Rib and work even until the piece measures approximately 10½ (10¾, 11¼, 11½, 12¼) in/26.5 (27, 28.5, 29, 31) cm from the beginning, ending after WS row.

Shape Armholes
Work double fully fashioned decreases each side (see Notes) on the next row, then work single fully fashioned decreases each side every row 3 times, then every other row 4 times—52 (56, 60, 64, 68) stitches remain.

Continue even in the pattern as established until the piece measures approximately 14 (14½, 15, 15½, 16½) in/35.5 (37, 38, 39.5, 42) cm from the beginning, ending after WS row.

Shape Neck
Next Row (RS): Work across the first 11 (12, 14, 15, 17) stitches, join a second ball of yarn and bind off the middle 30 (32, 32, 34, 34) stitches, work across to end the row.

Work both sides of the neck with separate balls of yarn and decrease 1 stitch each neck edge twice—9 (10, 12, 13, 15) stitches remain on each side.

Work both sides at once with separate balls of yarn until the piece measures approximately 15 (15½, 16, 16½, 17½) in/38 (39.5, 40.5, 42, 44.5) cm from the beginning.

Bind off.

FRONT
Same as the Back until piece measures approximately 12 (12½, 13, 13½, 14½) in/30.5 (32, 33, 34.5, 37) cm from the beginning, ending after WS row.

Shape Neck
Next Row (RS): Work across the first 18 (19, 21, 21, 22) stitches; join a second ball of yarn and bind off the middle 16 (18, 18, 22, 22) stitches, work across to end the row.

Work both sides at once with separate balls of yarn and bind off 3 stitches each neck edge once, bind off 2 stitches each neck edge once, then decrease 1 stitch each neck edge every other row 4 times—9 (10, 12, 10, 13) stitches remain each side.

Continue even until the piece measures 15 (15½, 16, 16½, 17½) in/38 (39.5, 40.5, 42, 44.5) cm from the beginning.

Bind off.

Finishing
Block pieces to finished measurements.

Sew right shoulder seam.

NECKBAND

With the RS facing, pick up and knit 92 (94, 94, 98, 98) stitches along the neckline.

Knit one row.

Purl one row.

Repeat the last 2 rows once more.

Bind off knitwise, allowing the edge to roll to the WS.

Sew the left shoulder seam.

ARMHOLE BANDS

With the RS facing, pick up and knit 56 (58, 58, 60, 62) stitches along the armhole.

Complete same as the neckband.

Repeat for the other armhole.

Sew the side seams, including the side of the armhole bands.

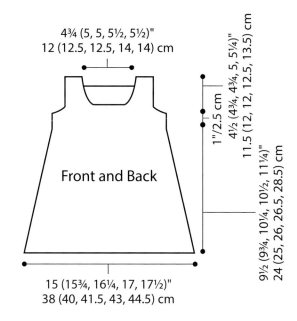

4¾ (5, 5, 5½, 5½)"
12 (12.5, 12.5, 14, 14) cm

1"/2.5 cm

4½ (4¾, 4¾, 5, 5¼)"
11.5 (12, 12, 12.5, 13.5) cm

Front and Back

9½ (9¾, 10¼, 10½, 11¼)"
24 (25, 26, 26.5, 28.5) cm

15 (15¾, 16¼, 17, 17½)"
38 (40, 41.5, 43, 44.5) cm

Nothing Beats Pleats

#InstaKnitsForBaby_NothingBeatsPleats

TIME TO KNIT 17 to 19 hours, depending on the size

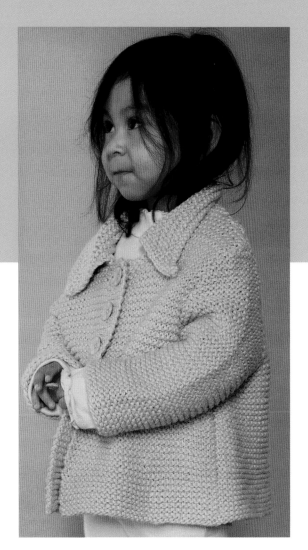

SIZES

6 Months (12 Months, 18 Months, 24 Months).
Instructions are for the smallest size, with
changes for other sizes noted in parentheses
as necessary.

FINISHED MEASUREMENTS

Chest: 21½ (24, 26½, 28) in/54.5 (61, 67.5, 71)
cm, buttoned
Length: 11 (12, 13, 14) in/28 (30.5, 33, 35.5) cm

MATERIALS

- Knitting Fever, Inc/Juniper Moon Farms
  Nimbus (#5 bulky weight; 96% Mako
  cotton/4% nylon; each approximately 3½
  oz/100 g and 164 yd/150 m), 3 (4, 4, 4) balls
  of Honeydew #07
- Knitting needles, US size 10½ (6.5 mm) or
  size needed to obtain gauge
- Double-pointed knitting needles, US size
  10½ (6.5mm) or size needed to obtain
  gauge
- 3 Buttons, ¾ in/20 mm diameter
- Stitch markers

GAUGE

In Garter Stitch, 17 stitches and 30 rows = 4
in/10 cm, blocked.

To save time, take time to check gauge.

Garter Stitch
Row 1 (RS): Knit across.

Pattern Row: As Row 1.

COAT

BACK

Cast on 78 (84, 90, 94) stitches.

Set Up Pattern

Row 1 (RS): K22 (25, 28, 30), place a marker, slip the next stitch purlwise (page 148) with the yarn in back, k7, p1, k16, p1, k7, slip the next stitch purlwise with the yarn in back, place a marker, k22 (25, 28, 30).

Row 2: K22 (25, 28, 30), slip the marker, p1, k7, slip the next stitch purlwise with the yarn in front, k16, slip the next stitch purlwise with the yarn in front, k7, p1, slip the marker, k22 (25, 28, 30).

Repeat the last 2 rows until the piece measures approximately 6 (6½, 7¼, 8) in/15 (16.5, 18.5, 20.5) cm from the beginning, ending after WS row.

Shape Armholes

Continue the pattern as established, bind off 2 (3, 4, 5) stitches at the beginning of the next 2 rows, bind off 2 (2, 3, 3) stitches at the beginning of the next 2 rows, then use the k2tog technique to decrease 1 stitch each side every row 2 (3, 2, 2) times—66 (68, 72, 74) stitches remain.

Continue even in the pattern as established until the piece measures approximately 9 (10, 11, 12) in/23 (25.5, 28, 30.5) cm from the beginning, ending after WS row.

Close the Pleat

Next Row (RS): Removing markers as you come to them, knit across to 9 stitches before the first marker, slip the next 8 stitches onto double-pointed needle #1, slip the next 8 stitches onto double-pointed needle #2, turn double-pointed needle #2 so that the wrong sides of fabric on both double-pointed needles face each other, position the 2 double-pointed needles in front of the left needle and [k3tog all 3 layers] 8 times; slip the next 8 stitches onto double-pointed needle #1, slip the next 8 stitches onto double-pointed needle #2, turn double-pointed needle #2 so that RS of fabric on both double-pointed needles face each other, position the 2 double-pointed needles behind the left needle so that WS of the stitches on double-pointed needle #2 and WS of the stitches on the left needle face each other, and [k3tog all 3 layers] 8 times—34 (36, 40, 42) stitches remain.

Continue even in Garter Stitch until the piece measures approximately 10½ (11½, 12½, 13½) in/26.5 (29, 32, 34.5) cm from the beginning, ending after WS row.

Shape Shoulders

Bind off 2 (2, 3, 3) stitches at the beginning of the next 6 rows, then bind off 3 (4, 3, 4) stitches at the beginning of the next 2 rows—16 stitches remain.

Bind off.

LEFT FRONT

Cast on 26 (28, 30, 33) stitches.

Begin Garter Stitch and work even until the piece measures the same as the back to armholes, ending after WS row.

Shape Armhole

Bind off 2 (3, 4, 5) stitches at the armhole edge once, bind off 2 (2, 3, 3) stitches at the armhole edge once, then use the k2tog technique to decrease 1 stitch at the armhole edge every row 2 (3, 2, 2) times—20 (20, 21, 23) stitches remain.

Continue even until the piece measures approximately 8½ (9½, 10½, 11½) in/21.5 (24, 26.5, 29) cm from the beginning, ending after RS row.

Shape Neck

Bind off 6 (5, 4, 5) stitches at the neck edge once, bind off 2 stitches at the neck edge once, then use the k2tog technique to decrease 1 stitch at the neck edge every row twice, then every other row once—9 (10, 12, 13) stitches remain.

Continue even until the piece measures the same as the back to shoulders, ending after WS row.

Shape Shoulder

Bind off 2 (2, 3, 3) stitches at the armhole edge 3 times.

Work 1 row even.

Bind off the remaining 3 (4, 3, 4) stitches.

Place markers for 3 buttons, making the first ¾ in/2 cm from the beginning of the front neck shaping, the third 4 in/10 cm from the beginning of the front neck shaping and the other one evenly spaced between the others.

RIGHT FRONT

Same as Left Front, except reverse all shaping and make buttonhole opposite markers on RS rows as follows: K3, bind off the next 2 stitches, knit across to end the row. On the subsequent row, cast on 2 stitches over the bound-off stitches.

SLEEVE (MAKE 2)

Cast on 32 (32, 34, 34) stitches.

Begin Garter Stitch, and use the kf&b (page 141) technique to increase 1 stitch each side every 8 rows 1 (2, 0, 0) times, every 10 rows 2 (2, 2, 0) times, every 12 rows 0 (0, 2, 3) times, then every 14 rows 0 (0, 0, 1) time—38 (40, 42, 42) stitches.

Continue even until the piece measures approximately 4¾ (5¾, 6¾, 7¾) in/12 (14.5, 17, 19.5) cm from the beginning, ending after WS row.

Shape Cap

Bind off 2 (3, 4, 5) stitches at the beginning of the next 2 rows, then use the k2tog technique to decrease 1 stitch each side every 4 rows 0 (0, 0, 2) times, every other row 7 (9, 9, 6) times, then every row 2 (0, 0, 0) times—16 stitches remain.

Work 0 (0, 1, 1) row even.

Bind off 2 stitches at the beginning of the next 4 rows—8 stitches remain.

Bind off.

Finishing

Block pieces to finished measurements.

Darn in yarn tails.

Sew the shoulder seams.

COLLAR

With WS facing, begin and end 1¾ in/4.5 cm in from front neck edge, pick up and knit 47 stitches along neckline.

Begin Garter Stitch, and use the K1f&b technique to increase 1 stitch each side every row until the collar measures approximately 1½ in/4 cm from the beginning, then increase 1 stitch each side every other row until the collar measures approximately 3 in/7.5 cm from the beginning.

Bind off.

Sew in sleeves.

Sew side and sleeve seams.

Sew on buttons opposite markers.

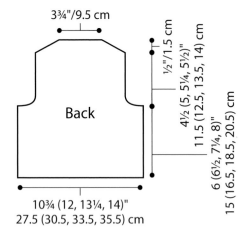

3¾"/9.5 cm

Back

½"/1.5 cm

4½ (5, 5¼, 5½)"
11.5 (12.5, 13.5, 14) cm

6 (6½, 7¼, 8)"
15 (16.5, 18.5, 20.5) cm

10¾ (12, 13¼, 14)"
27.5 (30.5, 33.5, 35.5) cm

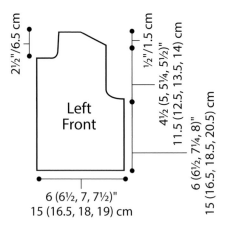

2½"/6.5 cm

Left
Front

½"/1.5 cm

4½ (5, 5¼, 5½)"
11.5 (12.5, 13.5, 14) cm

6 (6½, 7¼, 8)"
15 (16.5, 18.5, 20.5) cm

6 (6½, 7, 7½)"
15 (16.5, 18, 19) cm

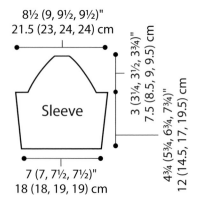

8½ (9, 9½, 9½)"
21.5 (23, 24, 24) cm

Sleeve

3 (3¼, 3½, 3¾)"
7.5 (8.5, 9, 9.5) cm

4¾ (5¾, 6¾, 7¾)"
12 (14.5, 17, 19.5) cm

7 (7, 7½, 7½)"
18 (18, 19, 19) cm

Note: Measurements are shown for the back after the pleat has been closed.

My Teddy Sweater

#InstaKnitsForBaby_MyTeddySweater

TIME TO KNIT **15 to 19 hours, depending on the size**

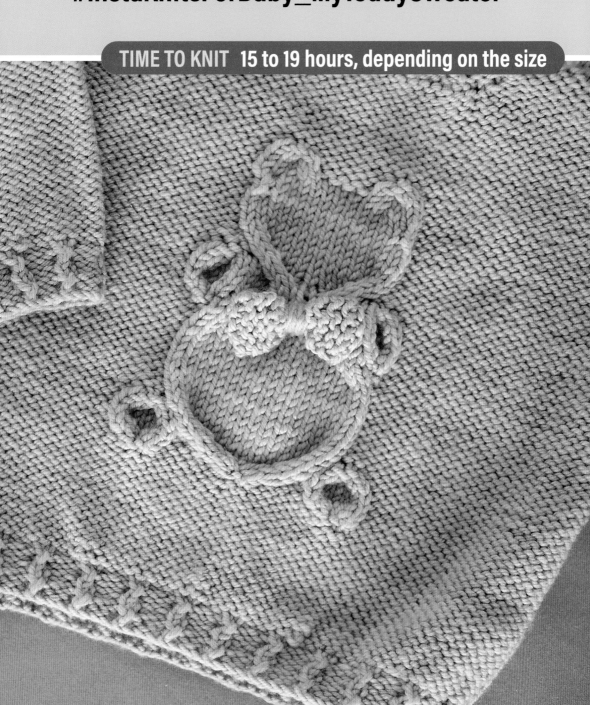

SIZES

6 Months (12 Months, 18 Months). Instructions are for the smallest size, with changes for other sizes noted in parentheses as necessary.

FINISHED MEASUREMENTS

Chest: 22 (24½, 27) in/56 (62, 68.5) cm
Length: 11 (12, 13) in/28 (30.5, 33) cm

MATERIALS

- Skacel/Hikoo *Sueño Worsted Tonal* (#4 medium weight; 80% superwash merino wool/20% bamboo; each approximately 3½ oz/100 g and 182 yd/166 m), 3 (3, 4) hanks of Succulent Tonal #1596
- Knitting needles, US size 7 (4.5 mm) or size needed to obtain gauge
- Knitting needles, US size 5 (3.75 mm)
- Cable needle
- 2 Stitch holders
- 4 Buttons, ½ in/10 mm diameter

GAUGE

In Reverse Stockinette with the larger needles, 18 stitches and 24 rows = 4 in/10 cm, blocked.

To save time, take time to check gauge.

Decorative Rib Pattern

Row 1 (RS): *P1, Right Twist (page 148), p1; repeat from the * across.

Row 2: *K1, p2, k1; repeat from the * across.

Row 3: *P1, Left Twist (page 139), p1; repeat from the * across.

Row 4: As Row 2.

Repeat Rows 1–4 for the pattern.

Reverse Stockinette

Row 1 (RS): Purl across.

Row 2: Knit across.

Repeat Rows 1 and 2 for the pattern.

Teddy Bear Motif (Over 19 Stitches, Increases to 37 Stitches)

See the chart on page 104 or refer to the text below.

Row 1 (RS): P1, [M1 (page 144), central double increase (page 136), M1, p7] twice, M1, central double increase, p1.

Row 2 and All WS Rows Except Rows 8, 26, and 40: Knit the knit stitches and purl the purl stitches.

Row 3: Slip the next stitch onto a cn and hold in back, k2, k1 from the cn, k1, slip the next 2 stitches onto a cn and hold in front, k1, k2 from the cn, p3, slip the next 3 stitches onto a cn and hold in back, k2, k3 from the cn, k1, slip the next 2 stitches onto a cn and hold in front, k3, k2 from the cn, p3, slip the next stitch onto a cn and hold in back, k2, k1 from the cn, k1, slip the next 2 stitches onto a cn and hold in front, k1, k2 from the cn.

Row 5: K7, slip the next 3 stitches onto a cn and hold in back, k2, k3 from the cn, k7, slip the next 2 stitches onto a cn and hold in front, k3, k2 from the cn, k7.

Row 7: Slip the next 2 stitches onto a cn and hold in front, p1, k2 from the cn, k1, slip the next stitch onto a cn and hold in back, k2, p1 from the cn, k17, slip the next 2 stitches onto a cn and hold in front, p1, k2 from the cn, k1, slip the next stitch onto a cn and hold in back, k2, p1 from the cn.

Row 8: K1, 5-to-1 Decrease (page 137), k1, p17, k1, 5-to-1 Decrease, k1.

Rows 9, 11, 13, and 15: P3, k17, p3.

Row 17: P3, slip the next 2 stitches onto a cn and hold in front, p1, k2 from the cn, k11, slip the next stitch onto a cn and hold in back, k2, p1 from the cn, p3.

Row 19: P3, M1, central double increase, M1, k15, M1, central double increase, M1, p3.

Row 21: P2, slip the next stitch onto a cn and hold in back, k2, k1 from the cn, k1, slip the

next 2 stitches onto a cn and hold in front, k1, k2 from the cn, k13, slip the next stitch onto a cn and hold in back, k2, k1 from the cn, k1, slip the next 2 stitches onto a cn and hold in front, k1, k2 from the cn, p2.

Row 23: P2, k27, p2.

Row 25: P2, slip the next 2 stitches onto a cn and hold in front, p1, k2 from the cn, k1, slip the next stitch onto a cn and hold in back, k2, p1 from the cn, k1, slip the next 3 stitches onto a cn and hold in back, k2, k3 from the cn, k1, slip the next 2 stitches onto a cn and hold in front, k3, k2 from the cn, k1, slip the next 2 stitches onto a cn and hold in front, p1, k2 from the cn, k1, slip the next stitch onto a cn and hold in back, k2, p1 from the cn, p2.

Row 26: K3, 5-to-1 Decrease, k1, p13, k1, 5-to-1 Decrease, k3.

Row 27: P4, slip the next 2 stitches onto a cn and hold in back, k2, k2 from the cn, k7, slip the next 2 stitches onto a cn and hold in front, k2, k2 from the cn, p4.

Rows 29 and 31: P4, k15, p4.

Row 33: P4, slip the next stitch onto a cn and hold in front, p1, k1 from the cn, k11, slip the next stitch onto a cn and hold in back, k1, p1 from the cn, p4.

Row 35: P4, Right Twist (page 148), k11, Left Twist (page 139), p4.

Row 37: P4, k3, slip the next stitch onto a cn and hold in back, k2, p1 from the cn, p3, slip the next 2 stitches onto a cn and hold in front, p1, k2 from the cn, k3, p4.

Row 39: P4, slip the next 2 stitches onto a cn and hold in front, p1, k2 from the cn, slip the next stitch onto a cn and hold in back, k1, p1 from the cn, p5, slip the next stitch onto a cn and hold in front, p1, k1 from the cn, slip the next stitch onto a cn and hold in back, k2, p1 from the cn, p4.

Row 40: K5, 3-to-1 Decrease (page 137), k7, 3-to-1 Decrease, k5.

SWEATER

BACK

With the smaller needles, cast on 48 (52, 60) stitches.

Begin the Decorative Rib Pattern, and work even for 8 rows.

Next Row (RS): Change to the larger needles, begin the Reverse Stockinette Pattern, and use the M1 purlwise (page 145) technique to increase 3 (5, 3) stitches evenly across the first row—51 (57, 63) stitches.

Continue even until the piece measures approximately 11 (12, 13) in/28 (30.5, 33) cm from the beginning, ending after WS row.

Next Row (RS): Bind off the first 35 (38, 43) stitches, then work across the remaining 16 (19, 20) stitches and slip them onto a holder.

FRONT

Same as the Back until 14 rows of Reverse Stockinette have been completed.

Setup Row (RS): Work across the first 16 (19, 22) stitches in Reverse Stockinette, place a marker, work Row 1 of the Teddy Bear Motif over the middle 19 stitches, place a marker, work Reverse Stockinette Stitch to end of row.

Slipping the markers as you come to them, work even until all 40 rows of the Teddy Bear Motif are complete.

Continue even in Reverse Stockinette Stitch over all stitches until the piece measures approximately 9½ (10½, 11½) in/24 (26.5, 29) cm from the beginning, ending after WS row.

Shape Neck

Next Row (RS): Work across the first 18 (21, 22) stitches; join a second ball of yarn and

bind off the middle 15 (15, 19) stitches, work across to end the row.

Work both sides at once with separate balls of yarn and use the k2tog decrease (page 143) and p2tog decrease (page 145) to decrease 1 stitch each neck edge every row twice—16 (19, 20) stitches remain each side.

Continue even, if necessary, until the piece measures 10¼ (11¼, 12¼) in/26 (28.5, 31) cm from the beginning, ending after WS row.

Next Row (RS): Slip first 16 (19, 20) stitches onto a holder for the buttonhole band; work across the remaining 16 (19, 20) stitches.

Continue even on this side until it measures approximately 11 (12, 13) in/28 (30.5, 33) cm from the beginning.

Bind off.

SLEEVE (MAKE 2)

With the smaller needles, cast on 28 (28, 32) stitches.

Begin the Decorative Rib Pattern and work even for 8 rows.

Next Row (RS): Change to the larger needles, begin the Reverse Stockinette Pattern and use the M1 purlwise technique to increase 3 (3, 1) stitch(es) evenly across the first row—31 (31, 33) stitches.

Continue in Reverse Stockinette and use the M1 purlwise to increase 1 stitch each side every other row 2 (1, 0) times, every 4 rows 5 (7, 6) times, then every 6 rows 0 (0, 2) times—45 (47, 49) stitches.

Continue even until the piece measures approximately 6½ (7½, 8) in/16.5 (19, 20.5) cm from the beginning.

Bind off.

Finishing
Block pieces to finished measurements.

BOWTIE
With the smaller needles, cast on 5 stitches.

Work in Garter Stitch (knitting every row) until the piece measures approximately 3½ in/9 cm from the beginning. Bind off.

Seam the cast-on and bound-off edges together.

With the seam to the WS, sew the bowtie onto the bear's neck, wrapping the yarn several times to create the middle of the bowtie as seen in the photo.

Sew right shoulder seam.

NECKBAND
With the RS facing and the smaller needles, pick up and knit 48 (48, 52) stitches along the neckline.

Next Row (WS): Work Row 2 of the Decorative Rib Pattern.

Next 2 Rows: Work Rows 3 and 4 of the Decorative Rib Pattern.

Next 4 Rows: Work Rows 1–4 of the Decorative Rib Pattern once more.

Bind off in the pattern.

BUTTON BAND
With the RS facing and smaller needles, pick up and knit 6 stitches along the side of neck-band, then slip 16 (19, 20) stitches from the back button band holder onto the needle and knit them, increasing 2 (3, 2) stitches evenly spaced as you knit—24 (28, 28) stitches.

Next Row (WS): Work Row 2 of the Decorative Rib Pattern.

Next Row: Work Row 3 of the Decorative Rib Pattern.

Next Row: Work Row 4 of the Decorative Rib Pattern.

Next Row: Work Row 1 of the Decorative Rib Pattern as you bind off.

Place markers for 4 evenly spaced buttons on band, making the first and last ¼ in/0.5 cm from side edges.

BUTTONHOLE BAND
With the RS facing and smaller needles, slip 16 (19, 20) stitches from the front buttonhole band holder onto the needle and knit them, increasing 2 (3, 2) stitches evenly spaced as you knit, then pick up and knit 6 stitches from the side of the neckband—24 (28, 28) stitches.

Next Row (WS): Work Row 2 of the Decorative Rib Pattern.

Next Row: Work Row 3 of the Decorative Rib Pattern and make buttonholes opposite markers on button band by working [k2tog, yarn over].

Next Row: Work Row 4 of the Decorative Rib Pattern.

Next Row: Work Row 1 of the Decorative Rib Pattern as you bind off.

Overlap the buttonhole band over the button band and sew the armhole ends together.

Place markers 4¾ (5, 5¼) in/12 (12.5, 13.5) cm down from the shoulders.

Set in the sleeves between markers.

Sew the sleeve and side seams.

Darn in all yarn tails.

Sew on buttons.

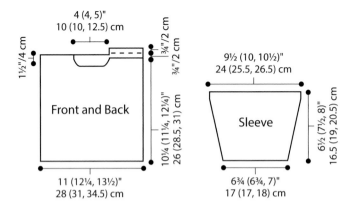

TEDDY BEAR MOTIF

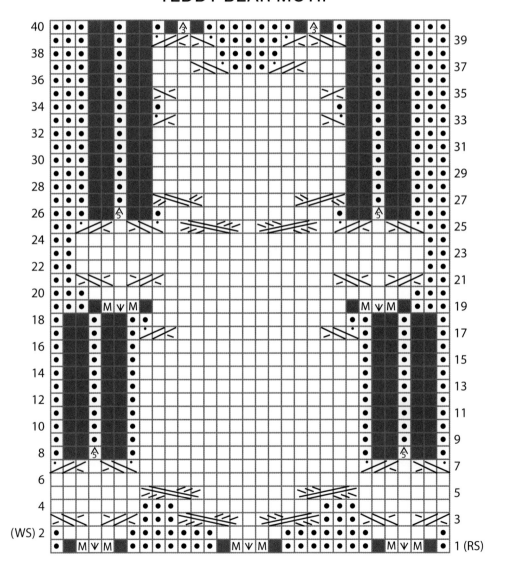

Symbol Key

☐ = On right-side rows: Knit
On wrong-side rows: Purl

• = On right-side rows: Purl
On wrong-side rows: Knit

■ = No stitch

M = M1 Knitwise = Insert the left-hand needle from front to back under the horizontal strand between 2 sts and knit it through its back loop

v = Central Double Increase = (Increases from 1 st to 3 sts) = Knit into the back and then into the front of the indicated st and slip these 2 new sts onto the right-hand needle; insert the point of the left-hand needle behind the vertical strand that runs downward between the 2 sts just made and knit into the front of it

⬆ = (Decreases from 5 sts to 1 st) = Slip the next 3 sts with the yarn in back, drop the yarn,
* pass the second st on the right-hand needle over the first st on the right-hand needle; slip the first st from the right-hand needle back to the left-hand needle; pass the second st on the left-hand needle over the first st on the left-hand needle, **slip the first st from the left-hand needle back to the right-hand needle and repeat from the * to the ** once more; pick up the yarn and knit the remaining st

⬆₃ = (Decreases from 3 sts to 1 st) = Slip the next 2 sts with the yarn in back, drop the yarn, pass the second st on the right-hand needle over the first st on the right-hand needle; slip the first st from the right-hand needle back to the left-hand needle; pass the second st on the left-hand needle over the first st on the left-hand needle, pick up the yarn and knit the remaining st

⤨ = Slip the next 3 sts onto cn and hold in back; k2; k3 from cn

⤨ = Slip the next 2 sts onto cn and hold in front; k3; k2 from cn

⤨ = Slip the next 2 sts onto cn and hold in back; k2; k2 from cn

⤨ = Slip the next 2 sts onto cn and hold in front; k2; k2 from cn

⤨ = Slip the next st onto cn and hold in back; k2; p1 from cn

⤨ = Slip the next 2 sts onto cn and hold in front; p1; k2 from cn

✕ = Right Twist = K2tog, leaving the sts on the left-hand needle, then insert the point of the right-hand needle between these 2 sts and knit the first one again

✕ = Left Twist = Skip the first st and k1-tbl, then knit the skipped st and slip both sts off the left-hand needle together

⤨ = Slip the next st onto cn and hold in back; k1; p1 from cn

⤨ = Slip the next st onto cn and hold in front; p1; k1 from cn

⤨ = Slip the next st onto cn and hold in back; k2; k1 from cn

⤨ = Slip the next 2 sts onto cn and hold in front; k1; k2 from cn

MORE THAN TWENTY HOURS

Planning on lounging at the pool on your next vacay? Pack your knitting bag so you can begin (and complete!) an awesome blanket for your Cutie!

#PoolsideKnitting
#KnittingOnVacation
#KnittedBabyBlankets

Giraffe Blankie

#InstaKnitsForBaby_GiraffeBlankie

TIME TO KNIT 21 hours

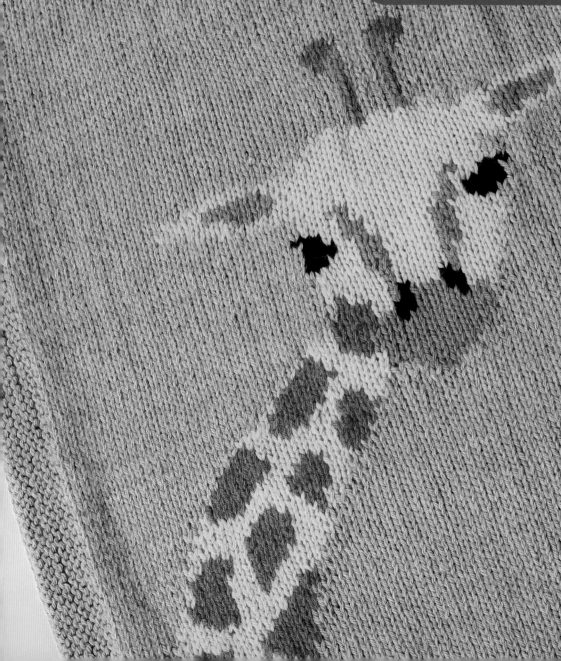

SIZES
One size

FINISHED MEASUREMENTS
36 × 37 in/91.5 × 94 cm

MATERIALS
- Berroco *Vintage Chunky* (#5 bulky weight; 52% acrylic/40% wool/8% nylon; each approximately 3½ oz/100 g; 136 yd/125 m), 5 hanks of Calico #6172 (A) and 1 hank each of Sunny #6121 (B), Pumpkin #6176 (C), Cork #6144 (D) and Cast Iron #6145 (E)
- Circular knitting needle, US size 10 (6 mm) or size needed to obtain gauge, 29 in/74 cm in length
- Stitch marker

GAUGE
In Stockinette Stitch, 14 stitches and 20 rows = 4 in/10 cm, blocked.

To save time, take time to check gauge.

Stockinette Stitch
Row 1 (RS): Knit across.

Row 2: Purl across.

Repeat Rows 1 and 2 for the pattern.

Garter Stitch
Row 1 (RS): Knit across.

Row 2: Knit across.

Repeat Rows 1 and 2 for the pattern.

BLANKET

With A, cast on 112 stitches.

Setup Row 1 (RS): With A, k46, place a marker, work Row 1 of the Giraffe Pattern across 66 stitches to end the row.

Continue even in Stockinette, working the 46 stitches in solid A and the 66 stitches in the Giraffe Pattern.

When Row 100 is completed, continue even with A until the piece measures approximately 32 in/81.5 cm from the beginning, ending after WS row.

Bind off.

Finishing

EDGING
With the RS facing and A, pick up and knit 112 stitches along one short side of the blanket.

Begin Garter Stitch, and use the M1 technique (page 144) to increase 1 stitch each side every other row 5 times—122 stitches.

Bind off.

Repeat for the second short side of the blanket.

With the RS facing and A, pick up and knit 126 stitches along one long side of the blanket.

Complete same as for the short side.

Repeat for the second long side of the blanket.

Sew the mitered corners.

Darn in all yarn tails (page 139).

Block to finished measurements.

Color Key

⬜	= A
⬜	= B
⬛	= C
⬛	= D
⬛	= E

GIRAFFE PATTERN

All Heart Blanket

#InstaKnitsForBaby_AllHeartBlanket

TIME TO KNIT 37 hours

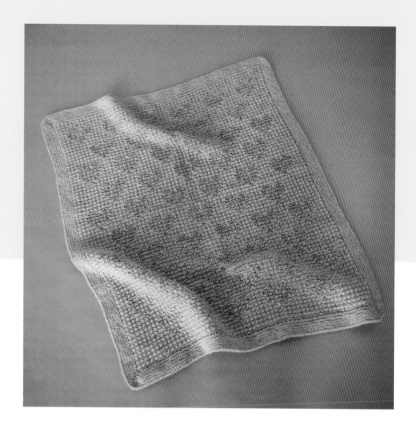

SIZES
One size

FINISHED MEASUREMENTS
30 × 36 in/76 × 91.5 cm

MATERIALS
- Lion Brand *Vanna's Choice* (#4 medium weight; 100% acrylic; 3 oz/85 g; each 145 yd/133 m), 5 hanks of Silver Heather #405 (A) and 3 hanks of Rose Mist #301 (B)
- Circular knitting needle, US size 10 (6 mm) or size needed to obtain gauge, 29 in/74 cm in length

GAUGE
In the Hearts Pattern, 17 stitches and 36 rows = 4 in/10 cm, blocked.

To save time, take time to check gauge.

NOTES:
- *Blanket is knit using just one color per row.*
- *Stitches are always slipped purlwise (page 150) with the yarn to the wrong side.*

BLANKET

With A, cast on 125 stitches.

Change to B and begin the Hearts Pattern.

Work Rows 1–4 3 times, then work Rows 5–60 5 times, then work Rows 61–64 3 times.

Bind off.

BORDER

With RS facing and A, pick up and knit 112 stitches along one short side of the blanket.

Begin Garter Stitch and use the M1 technique (page 144) to increase 1 stitch each side every other row 5 times—122 stitches.

Bind off.

Repeat for the second short side of the blanket.

With RS facing and A, pick up and knit 115 stitches along one long side of the blanket.

Complete same as for the short side.

Repeat for the second long side of the blanket.

Sew the mitered corners.

Darn in all yarn tails.

Stitch Key □ = Knit on RS; purl on WS

• = Purl on RS; knit on WS

∨ = Slip stitch purlwise with the yarn to the WS

Color Key ▢ = A

▢ = B

Hearts Pattern

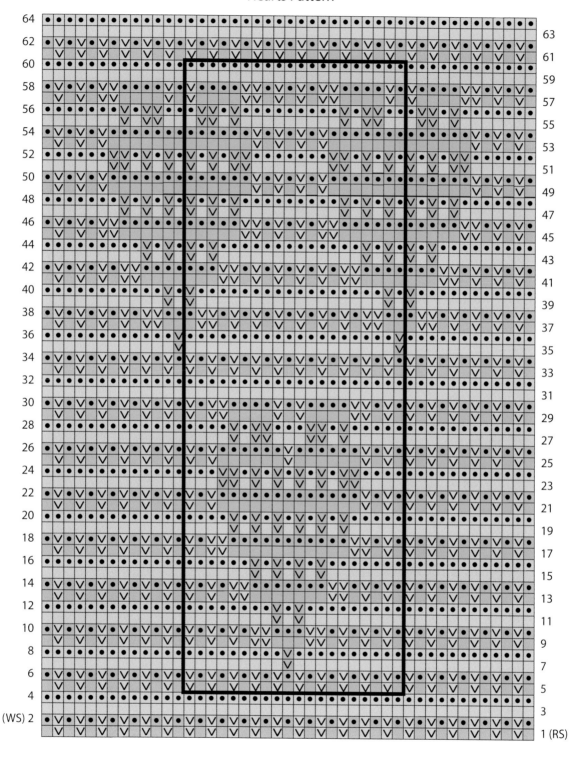

Cuddle-Up Throw

#InstaKnitsForBaby_CuddleUpThrow

TIME TO KNIT 38 hours

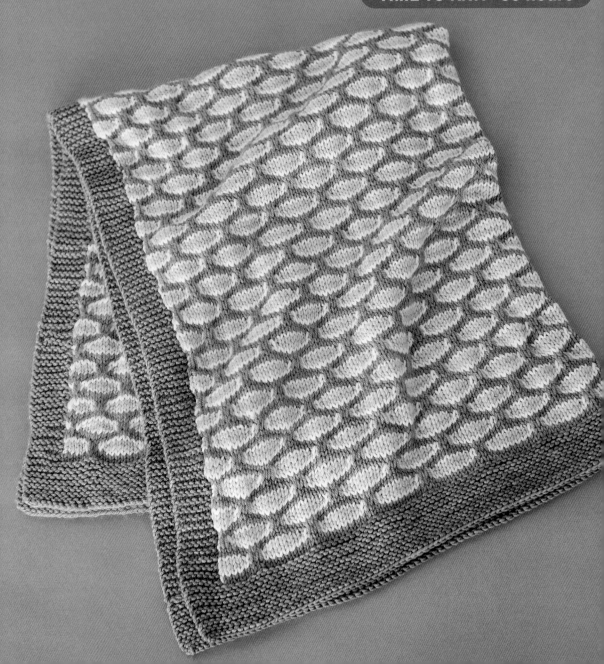

SIZES
One size

FINISHED MEASUREMENTS
32 × 39 in/81.5 × 99 cm

MATERIALS
- Manos del Uruguay *Alegria Grande* (#4 medium weight; 75% superwash merino wool/25% polyamide; 3½ oz/100 g and 219 yd/200 m), 3 hanks of Fern #2357 (A), 2 hanks of Natural #2800 (B), and 1 hank of Petal #2149 (C)
- Circular knitting needle, US size 8 (5 mm) or size needed to obtain gauge, 32 in/80 cm in length
- 2 Stitch markers

GAUGE
In the Slip Stitch, 22 stitches and 24 rows = 4 in/10 cm, blocked.

To save time, take time to check gauge.

NOTES:
- *Always slip stitches purlwise with the yarn to the wrong side (page 150).*
- *To keep the side edges in A, when working the main body of the blanket, use 2 balls of A, one for each side edge.*

Garter Stitch
Row 1 (RS): Knit across.

Row 2: Knit across.

Repeat Rows 1 and 2 for the pattern.

Slip Stitch Pattern (Multiple of 10 + 2 stitches)
Rows 1 and 7 (RS): With A, knit across.

Rows 2 and 8: With A, purl across.

Row 3: With B, k1, *k4, slip the next 2 stitches with the yarn in back, k4; repeat from the * across, ending with k1.

Row 4: With C, p1, *p3, slip the next 4 stitches with the yarn in front, p3; repeat from the * across, ending with p1.

Row 5: With C, k1, *k3, slip the next 4 stitches with the yarn in back, k3; repeat from the * across, ending with k1.

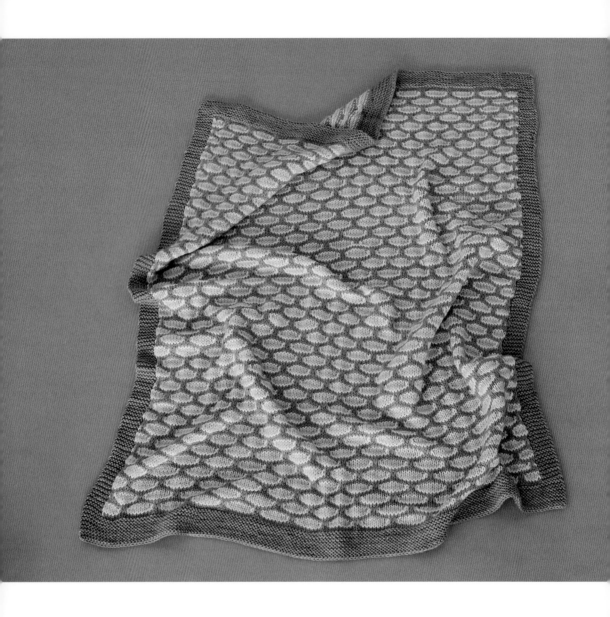

Row 6: With B, p1, *p4, slip the next 2 stitches with the yarn in front, p4; repeat from the * across, ending with p1.

Row 9: With B, k1, *slip the next stitch with the yarn in back, k8, slip the next stitch with the yarn in back; repeat from the * across, ending with k1.

Row 10: With C, p1, *slip the next 2 stitches with the yarn in front, p6, slip the next 2 stitches with the yarn in front; repeat from the * across, ending with p1.

Row 11: With C, k1, *slip the next 2 stitches with the yarn in back, k6, slip the next 2 stitches with the yarn in back; repeat from the * across, ending with k1.

Row 12: With A, p1, *slip the next stitch with the yarn in back, p8, slip the next stitch with the yarn in back; repeat from the * to the last stitch, ending with p1.

Repeat Rows 1–12 for the pattern.

BLANKET

With A, cast on 135 stitches.

Work 13 rows of Garter Stitch. Place markers to set off 7 stitches on each side.

Next Row (WS): Knit across, and use the M1 technique (page 144) to increase 21 stitches evenly spaced between the markers—156 stitches.

Slipping the markers as you come to them and keeping the first and last 7 stitches in Garter Stitch with A and the Slip Stitch Pattern over the middle 142 stitches, work even until the piece measures approximately 36½ in/92. 5 cm from the beginning, ending after Row 2 of the pattern.

Next Row (RS): With A, knit across, and use the k2tog technique (page 143) to decrease 21 stitches evenly spaced between the markers—135 stitches.

Work 13 rows of Garter Stitch.

Bind off.

Finishing
Darn in all yarn tails.

Block piece to measurements.

Slip Stitch Pattern

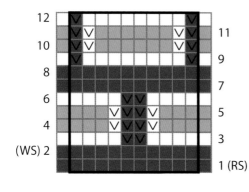

Color Key

■ = A

□ = B

▨ = C

Symbol Key

□ = Knit on RS; purl on WS

∨ = Slip the next stitch purlwise with the yarn to the wrong side of the fabric

Graceful Blanket

#InstaKnitsForBaby_GracefulBlanket

TIME TO KNIT 30 hours

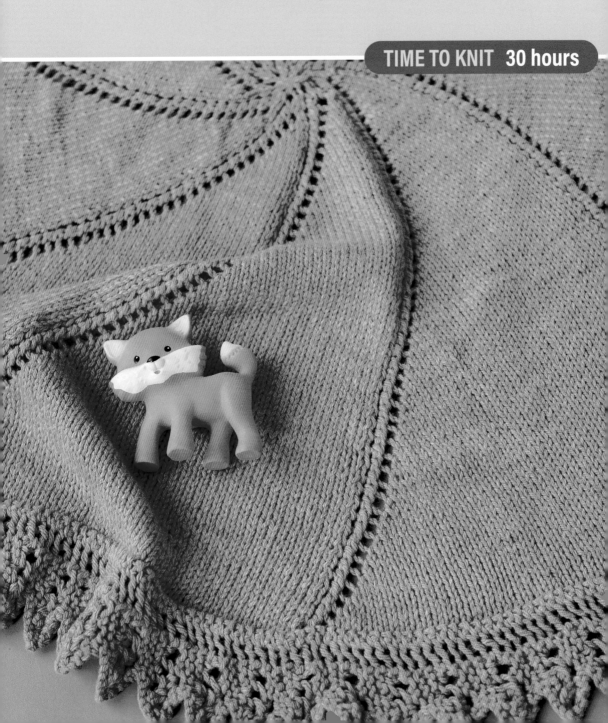

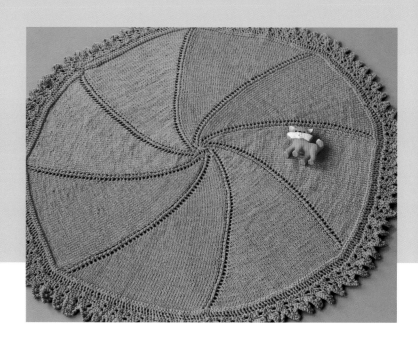

SIZES
One size

FINISHED MEASUREMENTS
46 in/117 cm in diameter

MATERIALS
- Berroco *Vintage Chunky* (#5 bulky weight; 52% acrylic/40% wool/8% nylon; each approximately 3½ oz/100 g and 136 yd/125 m), 7 hanks of Guava #61193
- Circular knitting needle, US size 9 (5.5 mm) or size needed to obtain gauge, 16 in/40 cm in length
- Circular knitting needle, US size 9 (5.5 mm) or size needed to obtain gauge, 29 in/74 cm in length
- 4 Circular knitting needles, US size 9 (5.5 mm) or size needed to obtain gauge, 40 in/102 cm in length
- Double-pointed knitting needles, US size 9 (5.5 mm) or size needed to obtain gauge
- 8 Stitch markers, with one in a contrasting color to indicate the beginning of the round

GAUGE
In Stockinette Stitch, 16 stitches and 20 rounds = 4 in/10 cm, blocked.

To save time, take time to check gauge.

Edging Pattern (Begins with 9 Stitches, Increases to 15 Stitches)

Row 1 (RS): Slip the first stitch knitwise (page 144), k2, yarn over, k2tog, [yarn over] twice, k2tog, [yarn over] twice, k2tog.

Row 2: [K2, p1] twice, k2, yarn over, k2tog, skp (page 143).

Row 3: Slip the first stitch knitwise, k2, yarn over, k2tog, k2, [yarn over] twice, k2tog, [yarn over] twice, k2tog.

Row 4: K2, [p1, k2] twice, k2, yarn over, k2tog, skp.

Row 5: Slip the first stitch knitwise, k2, yarn over, k2tog, k4, [yarn over] twice, k2tog, [yarn over] twice, k2tog.

Row 6: [K2, p1] twice, k6, yarn over, k2tog, skp.

Row 7: Slip the first stitch knitwise, k2, yarn over, k2tog, k10.

Row 8: Bind off the first 6 stitches, k5 additional stitches (6 knit stitches on needle), yarn over, k2tog, skp.

Repeat Rows 1–8 for the pattern.

BLANKET

Cast on 8 stitches.

Divide the 8 cast-on stitches evenly around 4 double-pointed needles. Join, taking care not to twist the stitches and place a marker for the beginning of the round.

Round 1 (RS): *K1, yarn over, place a marker; repeat from the * around—16 stitches.

Round 2 and All Even-Numbered Rounds: Knit around.

Round 3: *K1, yarn over, k1; repeat from the * around—24 stitches.

Round 5: *K1, yarn over, ssk (page 153), yarn over; repeat from the * around—32 stitches.

Round 7: *K1, yarn over, ssk, yarn over, k1; repeat from the * around—40 stitches.

Round 9: *K1, yarn over, ssk, yarn over, knit across to the next marker; repeat from the * around—48 stitches.

Round 10: As Round 2.

Repeat the last 2 rounds 45 *more* times—408 stitches (8 stitches are increased every 2 rounds).

Edging
Work a knit-on perpendicular edging, joining it to the live blanket stitches as follows:

With RS facing and using working yarn, cast 9 stitches onto a double-pointed needle; do not turn.

Using a second double-pointed needle, work Row 1 of the Edging Pattern.

Turn the blanket so that the WS is facing and the blanket is to the left of the edging on the double-pointed needle, ready to work a WS row. Transfer the edging stitches from the double-pointed needle to the left-hand tip of the circular needle, with the working yarn at the right of the edging stitches.

Work Row 2 (a WS row) of the Edging Pattern, joining the last edging stitch to the first live body stitch with an skp as indicated in the Edging Pattern; turn and work Edging Row 3, keeping all stitches on the circular needle.

Continue working the 8-row Edging Pattern along the edge of the body of the blanket, joining the last edging stitch on each WS row to the next live stitch until no more live body stitches remain.

Loosely bind off the remaining edging stitches.

Finishing
Sew the cast-on edge of the edging to the bound-off edge.

Darn in all yarn tails.

Block the piece to finished measurements, pinning out each point along the outer edge.

RESOURCES

This section includes information about knitting instructions and charts, the essentials for knitting techniques, the knitting community, and more.

READING KNITTING CHARTS AND PATTERNS

This book presents many stitch patterns in both text and chart form. Many knitters prefer using the graphics of the charts, but others like everything written out in text. Choose the format that makes your knitting easier and more fun.

KNITTING CHARTS

THE FOREIGN LANGUAGE OF KNITTING SYMBOLS AND CHARTS:

A Crash Course in Translation

To newbies, charted knitting patterns might seem like a secret code of cryptic characters laid out mysteriously on a grid. Actually, like foreign languages, knitting charts and their symbols are simple to translate once you become familiar with the "grammar" and "vocabulary."

A Quick Lesson in Grammar

A knitting chart is a visual representation of the public side of knitted fabric.

Each square of the grid corresponds to one stitch and each row of squares corresponds to one row (or round, if knitting circularly) of stitches.

Charts are read in the same way that the fabric is knit—from the lower edge up, with the first row at the bottom of the chart and the last row at the top.

Right-side rows are read from right to left, in the same order that stitches present themselves to you on the left-hand knitting needle. The following illustration shows the order that stitches will be worked for Row 1, a right-side row (the side of the fabric which the public will see), in a chart:

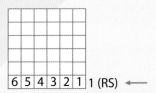

Of course, if you're knitting back and forth in rows, at the end of this first row, you flip your knitting before starting the next row, and the wrong side of the fabric faces you. Physically, the first stitch of this wrong-side row is the same stitch as the last stitch of the right-side row you just completed. Thus, wrong-side rows on charts are read in the opposite direction, from left to right, as shown below:

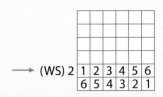

124

When working in-the-round rather than back-and-forth in rows, such as for a hat or sock, the right side of the fabric is always facing you so, in these cases, all rows of the chart are read from right to left.

Knitting charts make it easy to see how many stitches are involved in a pattern. A bold rectangular frame is used in this book to indicate the stitch repeat. If extra stitches are required on each side to center the pattern on the fabric, they are shown to the left and/or right of the repeat. The Slip Stitch Pattern that is used in the Cuddle-Up Throw on page 116 is a multiple of ten plus one stitches; it is a ten-stitch repeat with one selvedge stitch on each side.

To read the sample chart below, for example, you'd start at the lower right-hand corner, read from right to left, work the two stitches inside the bold rectangle as many times as is necessary to get across your fabric and end the row with the stitch represented in this sample chart by the star. This stitch sits outside the stitch repeat and so is worked once per row. It is the *last* stitch of every right-side row, and since wrong-side rows are read from left-to-right, it is the *first* stitch of every wrong-side row.

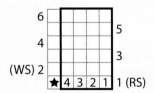

The Vocabulary List
Each symbol on a chart indicates the way a stitch or group of stitches will be worked, and the arrangement of symbols on the chart determines the stitch pattern.

Usually, the symbols visually resemble the way the resulting stitches will appear on the public side of the knitted fabric. The symbol for a knit stitch, for example, is a blank box, mimicking the flat appearance of the knit stitch itself; the

dot symbol for a purl stitch depicts the bumpy appearance of a purled stitch.

A symbol that occupies several squares of the grid indicates the number of stitches that will be involved in that particular knitting maneuver. Cables, for instance, are worked over more than one stitch, so cable symbols occupy several adjacent squares. In most of the charts in this book, each line or dot within every cable symbol represents one of the stitches being crossed, so you can quickly tell at a glance the number of stitches involved. For instance, two lines crossing two other lines would symbolize a four-stitch cable, such as in Row 27 of My Teddy Sweater on page 99.

Like the other knitting symbols used in charts, even cable symbols look like the knitting maneuvers they represent. In a Left Cross, the dominant lines in the symbol cross toward the left, with the right-hand stitches moving *in front* of the others. When knitting the symbol, this is your clue to place the cable needle holding those stitches *in front* of your work.

Left Cross

On the other hand, Right Cross cable symbols show the left-hand stitches moving over the others toward the right. Since the right-hand stitches appear to be moving *behind* the left-hand ones, you will slip them onto your cable needle and hold them *in back*.

Right Cross

When instructions say to hold yarn or stitches *in front* or *in back*, it means in front or in back of the piece of work as you see it on your needles. "In front" means the side you are looking at; "in back" means the side away from you at that time.

Needless to say, designers and editors may use different sets of symbols to represent the same knitting maneuvers, but they are usually "variations on a theme" and generally all symbols resemble the resulting stitch. Just think about them as unique "dialects" of this "foreign language"! They're usually pretty easy to decipher, since every chart has a key somewhere near it. The comprehensive glossary to all symbols used in this book is on page 129.

Conventional knitting charts show all rows in charts *as they appear on the public side of the* *fabric*. Therefore, the same symbol can mean different things on right-side and wrong-side rows. The blank box, for instance, represents a knit stitch on a right-side row, but if you're on a wrong-side row and want the stitch to appear as a knit stitch on the reverse side of the fabric, you must purl it.

If a symbol is used on both right- and wrong-side rows of the chart, the stitch glossary will tell you which knitting maneuver to use where.

KNITTING PATTERNS WRITTEN IN WORDS

Since some knitters prefer word-for-word patterns, every stitch pattern used in this book is written out in text form as well as chart format.

- Row-by-row instructions are typed out in numerical order. If the pattern has a repeat heightwise, the rows to be repeated will be indicated at the end of the pattern.
- As mentioned earlier, the "stitch multiple" indicates the number of stitches needed to repeat the pattern across the width of the fabric. In the text instructions, the stitch repeat is typed between the asterisk and semicolon. Any stitches outside the asterisk and semicolon are needed for symmetry.

- In the Garter Rib Pattern used in the Comfy Hoodie on page 58, for example, Row 1 reads like this:

  Row 1 (RS): *K1, p1; repeat from the * across, ending with k1.

To knit this row, you would alternately knit one stitch and then purl one stitch all the way across the row. At the end of the row, you will have one stitch remaining, and you will knit it. The extra knit stitch balances the pattern and makes it symmetrical.

- Instructions are written for the smallest size of each project with changes for larger sizes shown in parentheses as necessary.

ABBREVIATIONS

Following is a list of abbreviations used in the patterns of this book.

Many of the techniques are discussed in the Techniques section (pages 130–156).

cm	centimeter(s)
cn	cable needle
k	knit
kf&b	knit into the front and then the back of a stitch; this increases 1 stitch
k2tog	knit 2 stitches together as one; this is a right-slanting decrease
k3tog	knit 3 stitches together as one; this is a right-slanting double decrease
M1	make 1 knitwise or purlwise; this increases 1 stitch
mm	millimeter(s)
p	purl
p2tog	purl the next 2 stitches together as one stitch
RS	right side (of work)
s2kp2	slip next 2 stitches together knitwise, knit the next stitch, pass the 2 slipped stitches over the knitted stitch; this is a central double decrease
skp	slip the next stitch knitwise, knit the next stitch, pass the slipped stitch over the knitted stitch; this is a left-leaning decrease
ssk	slip the next 2 stitches knitwise, one at a time, from the left-hand needle to the right-hand one. Insert the left-hand needle tip into the fronts of both slipped stitches and knit them together from this position; this is a left-slanting decrease.
ssp	slip the next 2 stitches knitwise, one at a time, from the left-hand needle to the right-hand one. Return both stitches to left-hand needle and insert the right-hand needle into them from left to right and from back to front, then purl them together through their back loops; this is a left-slanting decrease.

sssk	slip the next 3 stitches knitwise, one at a time, from the left-hand needle to the right-hand one. Insert the left-hand needle tip into the fronts of all slipped stitches then knit them together from this position; this is a left-slanting double decrease.
st(s)	stitch(es)
tbl	through back loop
w&t	wrap and turn
WS	wrong side (of work)
*	repeat instructions after asterisk or between the asterisks across the row or for as many times as instructed.
[ ]	repeat the instructions within the brackets for as many times as instructed.
( )	instructions are written for the smallest size with changes for larger sizes inside the parentheses as necessary.

GLOSSARY OF CHART SYMBOLS

☐ = On right-side rows: Knit
On wrong-side rows: Purl

● = On right-side rows: Purl
On wrong-side rows: Knit

■ = No stitch

M = M1 Knitwise = Insert the left-hand needle from front to back under the horizontal strand between 2 sts and knit it through its back loop

Ⅴ = Central Double Increase = (Increases from 1 st to 3 sts) = Knit into the back and then into the front of the indicated st and slip these 2 new sts onto the right-hand needle; insert the point of the left-hand needle behind the vertical strand that runs downward between the 2 sts just made and knit into the front of it

⋀5 = (Decreases from 5 sts to 1 st) = Slip the next 3 sts with the yarn in back, drop the yarn, * pass the second st on the right-hand needle over the first st on the right-hand needle; slip the first st from the right-hand needle back to the left-hand needle; pass the second st on the left-hand needle over the first st on the left-hand needle, **slip the first st from the left-hand needle back to the right-hand needle and repeat from the * to the ** once more; pick up the yarn and knit the remaining st

⋀3 = (Decreases from 3 sts to 1 st) = Slip the next 2 sts with the yarn in back, drop the yarn, pass the second st on the right-hand needle over the first st on the right-hand needle; slip the first st from the right-hand needle back to the left-hand needle; pass the second st on the left-hand needle over the first st on the left-hand needle, pick up the yarn and knit the remaining st

= Slip the next 3 sts onto cn and hold in back; k2; k3 from cn

= Slip the next 2 sts onto cn and hold in front; k3; k2 from cn

= Slip the next 2 sts onto cn and hold in back; k2; k2 from cn

= Slip the next 2 sts onto cn and hold in front; k2; k2 from cn

= Slip the next st onto cn and hold in back; k2; p1 from cn

= Slip the next 2 sts onto cn and hold in front; p1; k2 from cn

= Right Twist = K2tog, leaving the sts on the left-hand needle, then insert the point of the right-hand needle between these 2 sts and knit the first one again

= Left Twist = Skip the first st and k1-tbl, then knit the skipped st and slip both sts off the left-hand needle together

= Slip the next st onto cn and hold in back; k1; p1 from cn

= Slip the next st onto cn and hold in front; p1; k1 from cn

= Slip the next st onto cn and hold in back; k2; k1 from cn

= Slip the next 2 sts onto cn and hold in front; k1; k2 from cn

Ⅴ = Slip stitch purlwise with the yarn to the WS

TECHNIQUES

This section provides instructions for the essential techniques used in the patterns, in alphabetical order.

ATTACHING NEW YARN

Whenever possible, try to attach a new ball of yarn at the beginning of a row.

To start a new strand of yarn at the beginning of a knit row: Drop the old yarn, insert your right needle into the first stitch of the row as if you are about to knit, grasp the new yarn, wrap it around the needle knitwise (page 144), and use it to knit the first stitch. Always begin and end every yarn with at least a 6 in/15 cm tail. Otherwise, you won't have enough length to weave it in sufficiently.

To start a new yarn at the beginning of a purl row: Drop the old yarn, insert your right needle into that first stitch of the row as if you're about to purl, wrap the yarn around the needle purlwise (page 148), and purl it. Again, be sure to leave a 6 in/15 cm tail.

BINDING OFF

Binding off is the technique that links all the live stitches together so they don't unravel when they are removed from the knitting needles. It is important to knit the knit stitches and purl the purl stitches as you come to them to prevent the edge from flaring out.

1. Begin by working 2 stitches in the pattern as established.

2. Use the tip of the left-hand needle to pull the first knitted stitch over the second one, removing this bound-off stitch from the right-hand needle.

3. To bind off another stitch, knit the next stitch, and use the tip of the left-hand needle to pull the first stitch on the right-hand needle over the second one.

4. Repeat these steps for each additional stitch being bound off.

BLOCKING

Prior to seaming your knitted pieces, take the time to block them into shape. You'll be surprised at how this simple process can improve the appearance of your projects and can tame even the most unruly stitches! To do it, follow the laundering instructions on the yarn label for the most delicate yarn in your project, then use rustless pins to shape the damp fabric to your desired measurements and allow it to dry. Or gently steam the pieces into shape by placing a damp cloth over them and then carefully wafting a hot steam iron just above the fabric. Don't actually touch the iron to the fabric or you'll risk flattening it.

BOBBLES

Bobbles introduce wonderful surface texture (not to mention, playful whimsy) to fabrics. While some knitters find them time-consuming to knit, they are not difficult to do. To make a bobble, multiple increases are worked into a single stitch, a few rows are worked, and then multiple decreases are worked to return to the original stitch count. Once the bobble is completed, simply work the rest of the row. There are several ways to knit a bobble, but here's my favorite. It is used in the cuff edge of the Elfin Booties on page 16.

1. Knit into the [front, back, front] of a single stitch, turn.

2. Working into these same 3 stitches, purl into the first one, [p1, yarn over, p1] *all into the next stitch*, then purl the third stitch, turn.

3. Knit the 5 stitches, then turn.

4. Decrease from 5 stitches to 3 stitches as follows: p2tog, p1, p2tog, turn.

5. Decrease from 3 stitches to 1 stitch using a central double decrease (also known as s2kp2) (page 152), then continue across the row.

CABLES

Cables are created when stitches exchange places with other stitches within a knitted row. One set of stitches is placed on a cable needle to keep them out of the way while another set of stitches is worked. Depending on whether those stitches are held to the front or to the back of the work, whether the cable uses two, three, or even seventeen stitches, and whether the stitches are ultimately knitted or purled or any combination of the two, creates the beautiful patterns.

Back Cross Cable (Also known as Right Cross)

1. Slip the first set of stitches purlwise onto a cable needle and hold them in the back.

2. Keeping the cable needle in back of work, knit the next set of stitches from the left needle.

3. Knit the set of stitches that is waiting on the cable needle.

4. Here's the finished cable crossing:

Front Cross Cable (Also known as Left Cross)

Work the same as the Back Cross Cable except hold the cable needle to the front of the work.

CAST ON

E-Wrap Cast-On

This method of adding stitches is used to make the buttonhole in the Rocking Horse Bib on page 63.

1. Begin with a slip knot, then use your thumb to twist the yarn to create a loop on the knitting needle as shown.

2. Continue in this way until the total number of stitches have been cast on.

Knit-On Cast-On

Here's my favorite cast-on method. It's beautiful, easy, and quick to do.

1. Start by making a slip knot as follows on one knitting needle.

2. Place the needle into your non-dominant hand and insert the tip of the empty needle knitwise (page 144) into the slip knot.

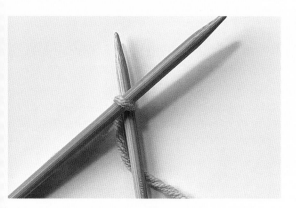

3. Wrap the yarn around the right needle to knit a stitch.

4. As you knit the new stitch, *don't remove the original stitch from the left needle*; instead, transfer the new stitch from the right needle back to the left one. One new stitch has been cast on.

5. For each successive stitch to be cast on, insert the right needle into the stitch just cast on and knit a stitch. As before, do not remove the old stitch, rather slip the new one back onto the left needle; repeat until you have cast on the required number of stitches.

CENTRAL DOUBLE INCREASE

This technique invisibly creates three stitches out of a single stitch and is used in My Teddy Sweater on page 99.

1. Begin by knitting into the back and then into the front of the indicated stitch, *in that order*, and then slip the 2 stitches off the left-hand needle and onto the right-hand needle.

3. Now, knit into this vertical strand *through its front loop*. Bingo! Three stitches have been made out of a single stitch.

2. To create the third stitch of this special increase, insert the left-hand needle *from back to front* into the little vertical strand that's beneath the two stitches just made. Just pull up on it a little to create enough space for your needle to fit.

FIVE-TO-1 DECREASE

This technique reduces five stitches to one stitch without any lumps and bumps. It is used in My Teddy Sweater on page 99. Work 3-to-1 Decrease the same way, except slip 2 stitches instead of 3 stitches in Step 1.

1. Drop the working yarn to the back and slip 3 stitches from the left needle onto the right needle purlwise.

2. *Pass the second stitch on the right needle over the first stitch as if you're binding it off.

3. Slip this stitch from the right needle back onto the left needle and pass the second stitch on the left needle over the first stitch (as if you're binding it off, except it will be in the opposite direction).

4. Now, slip this stitch from the left needle back onto the right needle* and repeat the steps between the 2 asterisks once more.

5. Finally, knit this remaining stitch. Five stitches have been combined into one stitch.

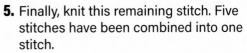

GAUGE

Gauge refers to the number of stitches and rows per inch of knitted fabric, and it reflects the size of each individual stitch. It is essential to understand how gauge works in order to control the finished size of your knitted projects.

Commercial patterns, including those in this book, are written for a particular gauge. For your finished project to be the same size as the one listed in the Finished Measurements section of the pattern and match the one photographed, you must consistently obtain the gauge called for, so be sure to measure your gauge correctly (and frequently!) as you work.

Often, patterns will indicate the desired gauge over 4 in/10 cm rather than over 1 in/2.5 cm. Since individual stitches tend to vary slightly in size, measuring over a larger width yields a more accurate determination of the gauge of the fabric.

Since blocking (page 132) tends to change the sizes of stitches, if you plan to block your project pieces, be sure to block your gauge swatch prior to measuring its gauge.

To accurately measure your gauge, knit a gauge swatch larger than 4 inches square in the stitch pattern used for the project, bind off all stitches, block, and then pin the fabric on a flat surface. Count the number of stitches over 4 in/10 cm, staying away from all edges of the fabric, and being careful not to press down too hard on the fabric, possibly distorting the stitches.

If you have fewer stitches per inch than what is specified in the pattern, then switch to smaller knitting needles; if you have more stitches, then switch to larger ones. Keep swatching, changing needle sizes until you obtain the gauge required.

Though often less crucial than stitch gauge, check your row gauge the same way, counting the number of rows instead of stitches.

HIDING YARN TAILS

Take the time to darn yarn tails the professional way! Use a pointed-end yarn needle to make short running stitches on the wrong side of your fabric in a diagonal line for about one inch or so, piercing the yarn strands that comprise the stitches of your fabric. Then, work back again to where you began, working alongside your previous running stitches. Finally, to secure the tail, work a stitch or two and actually pierce the running stitches you just created. Be sure to work each tail individually in opposite diagonal directions, and you will secure your yarn ends while keeping the public side of your fabric neat and beautiful.

INTARSIA

With this technique, the fabric appears to be stamped with a colorful graphic, but the picture is knitted right in!

Each section of color uses its own ball of yarn; the technique does not create floats on the WS.

To prevent holes, it is important to interlock the yarns as they meet. Here's how:

Drop the old yarn *to the left* of the new one and pick up the new one *from underneath* the old one, thereby crossing the yarn and begin knitting or purling.

LEFT TWIST

This technique simulates a tiny cable that is crossing to the left.

1. Skip first stitch on the left needle and with the right needle behind the left one, knit next stitch *in its back loop*.

2. Knit the first stitch in its front loop the regular way and then slip both stitches off the left needle together.

KNIT STITCH

The knit stitch is the most basic of all stitches. Here's how to do it:

1. Hold the needle with the cast-on stitches in your left hand with the tip pointing to the right. The yarn attached to the ball will be hanging off the right end of the needle.

2. With the working yarn in the back, insert the tip of the right needle from *front to back* into the first stitch on the left needle from the left to the right.

3. Wrap the yarn around the right needle from right to left, first under and then over the top of the right needle.

4. Use the right needle to scoop up the yarn and pull it toward you through the first stitch on the left needle.

5. Slide the original stitch off the left needle, keeping the new stitch on the right needle.

KNIT INTO THE FRONT AND BACK OF A STITCH (KF&B)

This type of increase adds a bit of horizontal texture that looks very much like a purl bump. It is easy to work and is often used when knitting ribbings, since it serves to incorporate new stitches into the pattern quickly.

1. To do in a knit stitch: insert the right needle into the indicated stitch knitwise (page 144), wrap the working yarn around the needle the regular way to knit a stitch *but don't remove the original stitch from the left needle.*

3. Two stitches are made out of one stitch.

2. Reinsert your right needle knitwise into the back of the same stitch, wrap the yarn around the needle to knit a stitch, then slip the original stitch off.

KNITTING IN THE ROUND

Sometimes, like when making the Lamb Hat on page 19 or the Preppy Socks on page 8, you'll want to create a tube of knitted fabric, eliminating the need for seams. Depending on the circumference of the knitting, you'll use one of the following methods.

Knitting in the Round on a Circular Knitting Needle

1. Simply cast on the required number of stitches onto the circular needle.

2. Take the time to ensure that the cast-on stitches are not twisted by checking to see that the nubby edge of every stitch is pointing toward the center.

3. Hold the circular needle so that the last cast-on stitch is near the tip of the needle in your right hand and the first cast-on stitch is near the tip of the needle in your left hand. To join the stitches into a circle to begin knitting in the round, knit the first stitch on the left needle, pulling tightly on the yarn to prevent a gap. Most knitters put a stitch marker on the needle to indicate the beginning of the round.

Knitting in the Round on Double-Pointed Knitting Needles

Since circular knitting needles don't come in small enough lengths to comfortably knit projects such as mittens or the crowns of hats, double-pointed knitting needles are used.

1. To start, cast on the required number of stitches onto a circular or straight knitting needle that is the same diameter as the double-pointed needles you'll be using.

2. For the first round of knitting, knit approximately one-fourth of the total number of stitches from the circular needle onto each double-pointed needle in succession.

3. Then, form a square out of the 4 needles, positioning the nubby edge of all the stitches toward the center to make sure the cast-on edge isn't twisted.

4. With the empty 5th needle, knit the first cast-on stitch, pulling tightly on the yarn to prevent a gap.

5. After working all stitches on the first needle, the empty needle becomes the working needle and you move on to work the stitches on the next needle. Continue in this way to the end of the round.

NOTE: *Because a beginning-of-the-round stitch marker will slip off the tip of the first needle, many knitters place it between the first and second stitch of the round.*

KNIT TWO TOGETHER DECREASE (K2TOG)
(RIGHT-SLANTING DECREASE)

1. With the working yarn toward the back, insert the right needle knitwise (page 144) into the first 2 stitches on the left needle as if they were a single stitch.

2. Wrap the yarn around the right-hand needle as you would for a knit stitch. Pull the yarn through both stitches and slip both stitches off the left needle at once. One stitch has been decreased and the resulting stitch slants to the right.

Designer Tip: See page 153 for the ssk decrease, the mirror image of the k2tog decrease.

KNITWISE

Instructions will sometimes tell you to insert your knitting needle into a stitch knitwise. To do this, simply insert the tip of your right-hand needle into the indicated stitch as if you were about to knit that stitch—in other words, from left to right and *from front to back*.

If you're told to *slip a stitch knitwise*, insert the tip of your right needle into the front of the stitch as if you're about to knit it and slide that stitch off the left-hand needle and onto the right one, allowing the stitch to sit on the right needle with its left "leg" in the front. Usually, stitches are slipped knitwise during a decrease.

MAKE 1 (M1) (ALSO KNOWN AS MAKE 1 KNITWISE)

This method of adding stitches uses the horizontal strand of yarn that hangs between the knitting needles. The knitter works into the strand, carefully twisting it to prevent a hole.

1. Use the left-hand needle to lift up the horizontal strand that's hanging between the needles, *from front to back*.

2. Knit the strand *through its back loop*, twisting it to prevent a hole in your fabric.

MAKE 1 PURLWISE (M1 PURLWISE)

Sometimes increases are worked as purl stitches. Here's how:

1. Use the left-hand needle to lift up the horizontal strand between the needles *from front to back*.

2. Then purl the strand *through its back loop*, twisting it to prevent a hole in your fabric.

PURL 2 TOGETHER DECREASE (P2TOG)

This method decreases two purl stitches down to a single stitch.

1. With the working yarn toward the front, insert the tip of the right needle into the first 2 stitches on the left needle purlwise (page 148) as if they were a single stitch.

2. Wrap the yarn around the right needle as you would for a purl stitch, pull the yarn through both stitches, and then slip both stitches off the left-hand needle at once. One stitch has been decreased and the resulting stitch slants to the right on the knit side of the fabric.

PICKING UP STITCHES

Most neckline treatments require that stitches be picked up along the neck opening. Here's how.

Picking Up Stitches along a Horizontal Edge

1. With RS of fabric facing you, insert a knitting needle *into the middle* of the first stitch just below the bind-off. Be sure to go into the center of the V, not into the links of the chain running along the top of the fabric.

2. Next, wrap the yarn around the needle knitwise (page 144) and use the tip of the needle to pull up a loop, creating a new stitch.

3. Use this method to pick up 1 stitch in each stitch across.

Picking Up Stitches along a Vertical Edge

1. With RS facing you, insert a knitting needle *between the first and second stitches* in the first row of knitting. Be sure to insert the needle *between* 2 stitches, not in the middle of a V.

2. Wrap the yarn around the needle knitwise (page 144), and use the tip of the needle to pull up a loop, creating a new stitch, just like Step 2 for Picking Up Stitches along a Horizontal Edge.

3. Use this method to pick up stitches along the edge, picking up 3 stitches out of every 4 rows for the correct ratio of stitches to rows.

Picking Up Stitches along a Curved Edge

When picking up stitches along the curved sections of a neckline, use the same method described above and be sure to insert your knitting needle inside the edge in order to hide any unevenness.

Designer Tip: Try to avoid picking up stitches in obvious holes in your fabric as this will make the holes look larger rather than hiding them.

PURL STITCH

This common stitch is the flip side of a knit stitch.

1. With the working yarn in the front, insert the tip of the right needle into the first stitch on the left needle *from back to front and from right to left*.

2. Wrap the yarn over and then under the right needle, returning the yarn to the original position.

3. Use the right needle to catch the yarn and draw it through the first stitch on the left needle, pushing the right needle from front to back.

4. Slip the original stitch off the left needle, keeping the new stitch on the right needle.

PURLWISE

When instructed to insert your knitting needle into a stitch purlwise, simply insert the tip of your right-hand needle into the indicated stitch as if you were about to purl that stitch—in other words, from right to left and *from back to front*.

RIGHT TWIST

This is the mirror image of the Left Twist (page 139). Here's how to work this little cable:

1. Knit 2 stitches together the regular way but do not remove them from the left needle.

2. Knit the first stitch again *through its front loop* and slip both stitches off the left needle together.

SEAMING

For most seams, I prefer using the mattress stitch technique as it is completely invisible. Here's how to do it both horizontally (stitch-to-stitch) and vertically (row-to-row):

Horizontal Seam

1. Lay your blocked pieces (page 132) flat with RS of the fabric facing you and with the bound-off edges of the pieces together.

2. Bring the needle up through the center of a stitch just below the bound-off edge on the lower piece of fabric, then insert it *from front to back* and from right to left around both legs of the corresponding stitch on the other piece of fabric.

3. Bring the needle tip back down through the center of the same stitch where it first emerged.

4. Continue this way until your seam is complete.

Vertical Seam

1. Lay your blocked pieces (page 132) flat, with RS of the fabric facing you, matching patterns and stripes, if applicable.

2. Thread a blunt-end yarn needle with your sewing yarn, then bring the needle up *from back to front* through the left-hand piece

of fabric, going in 1 stitch from the edge, leaving a 6 in/15 cm tail.

3. Bring the yarn up and through the corresponding spot on the right-hand piece to secure the lower edges.

4. Insert the needle *from front to back* into the same spot on the left-hand piece where the needle emerged last time and bring it up through the corresponding place of the next row of knitting.

5. Insert the needle *from front to back* into the same spot on the right-hand piece where the needle emerged last time and bring it up through the corresponding place of the next row of knitting.

6. Repeat the last 2 steps until you've sewn approximately 2 in/5 cm, then pull firmly on the sewing yarn to bring the pieces of the fabric together, allowing the 2 stitches on the edges of each piece to roll to the wrong side.

7. Continue this way until your seam is complete.

SLIDING STITCHES

Occasionally, such as when making I-cord, rather than turning at the end of a row, patterns will instruct you to slide the stitches to the beginning of the row. It is necessary to be working with a circular knitting needle or double-pointed knitting needles so you can knit off both ends. Here's how:

1. Complete a row.

2. Rather than turning the work, slide the stitches back to the tip of the needle where the last row was started and knit again as directed.

SLIPPING STITCHES

Interesting texture and colorwork can be created simply by slipping stitches from the left needle to the right one intermittently in a pattern. Sometimes the stitches are moved with the yarn toward the front of the stitch and other times toward the back. Here's the difference:

Slipping Stitches with Yarn in Back
When instructed to hold the yarn in back, slip the stitch onto the right needle purlwise (see page 148), keeping the working yarn behind the fabric *as it faces you*. The yarn will be toward the wrong side of the fabric if you are on a right-side row and toward the public side (RS) of the fabric if you're on a wrong-side row.

Slipping Stitches with Yarn in Front

To slip a stitch with the yarn in front, if the working yarn is not already in front of the fabric (toward you, such as when purling), bring it forward and slip the stitch. The yarn will be toward the public side (RS) of the fabric if you are on a right-side row and toward the wrong side of the fabric if you're on a wrong-side row.

NOTE: *When moving the yarn from front to back or from back to front, be careful to always bring it between the points of the knitting needles and not over the right needle. Otherwise, a yarn over will be created, increasing your stitch count and making an unexpected hole in your fabric.*

SLIP 1, KNIT 1, PASS THE SLIPPED STITCH OVER (SKP)

This is a left-slanting decrease. Here's how to do it:

1. Slip a stitch knitwise (page 144).

2. Knit the next stitch.

3. Pass the slipped stitch over the knitted stitch as if you are binding it off.

SLIP 2, KNIT 1, PASS THE 2 SLIPPED STITCHES OVER (S2KP2, CENTRAL DOUBLE DECREASE)

Here's a central double decrease that reduces 3 stitches to 1 stitch, leaving the center stitch on top.

1. Slip 2 stitches at once *knitwise*.

3. Finally, pass the 2 slipped stitches over the stitch you just knit.

2. Knit the next stitch.

4. Three stitches have been decreased to 1 stitch and the resulting stitch has no apparent slant.

SLIP, SLIP, KNIT DECREASE
(SSK, LEFT-LEANING DECREASE)

This knit decrease requires an extra step, but it creates a mirror image of the k2tog decrease described above.

1. With the working yarn toward the back, slip the next 2 stitches, *knitwise*, and *one at a time*, onto the right-hand needle.

2. Insert the tip of the left-hand needle into the fronts of both slipped stitches and knit them together from this position, through their back loops, wrapping the yarn around the right-hand needle, which is in the back.

3. One stitch has been decreased, and the resulting stitch slants to the left.

SLIP, SLIP, SLIP, KNIT DECREASE
(SSSK, LEFT-LEANING DOUBLE DECREASE)

Same as the ssk decrease (page 153), except 3 stitches are slipped knitwise, one at a time and then are knitted together from their new positions. Two stitches are decreased, and the resulting stitch slants to the left.

SLIP, SLIP, PURL DECREASE (SSP)

This technique is often used on wrong-side rows to mimic the left-slanting look of the ssk decrease on the knit side (RS) of the fabric.

1. With the working yarn toward the front, slip the first 2 stitches knitwise, one at a time, from the left needle to the right needle.

2. Slip these 2 stitches back to the left needle in their twisted position.

3. Insert the tip of the right needle into the back loops of these 2 stitches, going into the second stitch first and then the first stitch, and purl them together through their back loops as if they were a single stitch. One stitch has been decreased, and the resulting stitch leans toward the left on the knit side of the fabric.

THREE NEEDLE BIND-OFF

This technique uses knitting to seam live stitches together. It is used to finish the head of the Teddy Lovey on page 54 and the Koala Lovey on page 73.

1. To knit this type of seam, hold the 2 pieces of fabric with wrong sides together in your left hand.

2. Insert a third knitting needle knitwise (page 144) into the first stitch on each needle, 2 stitches on the needle.

3. Knit these 2 stitches together as if they're 1 stitch.

4. Slip the new stitch off onto the third needle.

5. Insert the third needle knitwise into the next 2 stitches on the left needles and knit them together, slipping the new stitch off onto the right needle.

6. Pass the first stitch on the right needle over the next stitch to bind it off.

7. Continue across the row, knitting together 1 stitch from each needle and binding off as you go.

WRAP AND TURN (W&T)

This technique is used in the Bonny Bib on page 29 and in the Graceful Blanket on page 120 to prevent holes when working short rows.

Here's how to do it: Bring the working yarn to the front, slip the next stitch purlwise onto the right needle, move the working yarn to the back, slip the stitch from the right needle back onto the left needle, bring the working yarn to the front and turn, leaving the rest of the row unworked.

1. Bring the working yarn to the front.

2. Slip the next stitch purlwise (page 148) onto the right needle.

3. Move the working yarn to the back.

4. Slip the stitch from the right needle back onto the left needle.

5. Bring the working yarn to the front and turn, leaving the rest of the row unworked.

YARN OVER INCREASE

This method of increasing places a decorative eyelet hole in the fabric just below the new stitch.

1. Bring the working yarn to the front between the tips of the two knitting needles.

2. As you knit the next stitch, the yarn will go over the right needle to create the extra stitch.

YARN CHOICE AND SUBSTITUTION

Every project in this book was designed for a specific yarn. Each yarn possesses its own characteristics, which will affect the way it appears and behaves when knitted. To duplicate the projects exactly as photographed, I suggest that you use the designated yarns. Even so, you'll find that the nature of any handmade garment assures subtle differences and variances.

However, if you would like to make a yarn substitution, be sure to choose one of similar weight to the one called for in the pattern. Yarn sizes and weights are usually located on the label, but for an accurate test, knit a swatch of stockinette stitch using the recommended needle size, making it at least 4 in/10 cm square.

Count the number of stitches in this 4 in/10 cm swatch and refer to the table below to determine the yarn's weight.

Yarn Size and Weight	Description	Stitches per 4 in/10 cm in Stockinette Stitch
1-Super Fine	Fingering weight	27 or more stitches
2-Fine	Sock weight	23–26 stitches
3-Light	DK weight	21–24 stitches
4-Medium	Worsted weight	16–20 stitches
5-Bulky	Bulky weight	12–15 stitches
6-Super Bulky	Super Bulky weight	11 or fewer stitches

MATERIAL RESOURCES

I always recommend purchasing supplies at your local yarn shop. If there isn't one in your area, contact the appropriate wholesaler below for more information.

Anzula Yarn
anzula.com

Berroco Yarn
berroco.com

Cascade Yarns
cascadeyarns.com

Knitting Fever, Inc./Juniper Moon Farm
knittingfever.com/brand/juniper-moon-farm
/yarns

Koigu Yarns
koigu.com

Lion Brand Yarn
lionbrand.com

Manos del Uruguay Yarns
manos.uy/yarns

Skacel Yarns
skacelknitting.com

Universal Yarn
universalyarn.com

THE KNITTING COMMUNITY

For more learning, inspiration, and fun, check out:

- education.pattylyons.com
- verypink.com
- ggmadeit.com
- knitty.com
- moderndailyknitting.com

- ravelry.com
- rowhouseyarn.com
- kateatherley.com
- vogueknittinglive.com
- tkga.org

AUTHOR RESOURCES

Follow me on Instagram @melissa.leapman for a sneak peek into my world.

Join my fan group on Ravelry to share photos of your projects and to keep up with my work.

Go to ravelry.com/groups/melissa-leapman -rocks and be part of the fun!

Head over to my website, MelissaLeapman. com, to sign up for my newsletter and be the first to hear about live KNITopia[SM] knitting events, cruises, virtual classes, knitalongs, and more!